Contents

Introduction

About this guide

This unit guide is for students following the OCR AS Sociology course. It deals with Module 2534 **Sociological Research Skills** and Module 2535 **Research Report (Sociology)**. Module 2534 is examined as a written paper and Module 2535 is the coursework alternative. Both modules are designed to give you a basic introduction to concepts such as reliability, validity, representativeness and generalisability, and issues in research design and evaluation such as sampling. This book aims to give you the skills to think through a range of research-based problems and to interrogate different types of sociological evidence associated with sociological enquiry.

There are four sections:

- **Introduction** — this provides guidance on how to use this unit guide, an explanation of the skills required in AS Sociology, the criteria that will be used to assess your grades, guidance on effective revision for the written examination and advice on how to complete the coursework successfully.
- **Content Guidance** — this provides an outline of what is included in the specifications of the Sociological Research Skills/Research Report modules. Candidates who choose to take the coursework option are required to study the same content as those taking the written examination. Guidance is given on how to tackle the coursework with details of the key areas to revise for the exam.
- **Questions and Answers** — this provides some exam-type questions for the Sociological Research Skills exam, together with some sample answers at grade-A and grade-C level. Examiner's comments are included to give you an insight into how the marks are awarded.
- **AS Coursework: The Research Report** — this gives you one example of coursework at grade-A and one at grade-C level. Your teacher marks the coursework and the examination board moderates the marks. Examiner/moderator comments are included on how the marks are awarded.

How to use the guide

Read this introduction thoroughly and ensure that you know what skills the examiners and moderators are looking for. Then, as you do your class work, keep returning to the skills section and ensure that you are demonstrating the ones that are required. Knowing what examiners are looking for and then practising those skills is one of the keys to success. The Content Guidance section gives you more detail about the bullet points in the specification — in other words, it tells you what you need to know to be certain you have covered the necessary material. Remember that exam questions can be set on any aspect of the specification, so you must ensure that you have covered all of the bullet points for each topic area you are studying. The Content

27466

AS Sociology
UNIT 3

Please return this book to
LRC ABERDARE CAMPUS
COLEG MORGANNWG
01685 887500 ext.192

Module 2534: Sociological Research Skills

Module 2535: Research Report

Viv Thompson

Series Editor: Steve Chapman

For Sarah and Danny with my love.

To the year 13 students at Oakbank School, especially Andrew and Jenny: thank you for 2 great years of sociology.

To Steve: for creating opportunities and being so supportive.

Philip Allan Updates
Market Place
Deddington
Oxfordshire
OX15 0SE

tel: 01869 338652
fax: 01869 337590
e-mail: sales@philipallan.co.uk
www.philipallan.co.uk

This Guide has been written specifically to support students preparing for the OCR AS Sociology Unit 3 examination. The content has been neither approved nor endorsed by OCR and remains the sole responsibility of the author.

Typesetting: Good Imprint, East Grinstead, West Sussex
Printed by Information Press, Eynsham, Oxford

Guidance section also gives you some important concepts associated with the topic of Sociological Research Skills, but it is important to remember that these are meant only as a guide — you will almost certainly come across others.

Read the relevant parts of the guide as you study the module. In order to get full advantage from the Question and Answer section, wait until you have completed your study of the topic, as the questions are wide-ranging. When you are ready to use this section, take each question in turn, study it carefully and either write a full answer or, at the very least, answer parts (a), (b) and (c) and write a plan for part (d). When you have done this, study the grade-A candidate's answer and compare it with your own, paying close attention to the examiner's comments. You could also look at the grade-C answers and, using the examiner's comments as a guide, work out how to rewrite them to gain higher marks. Just reading through the grade-A candidates' answers should provide you with useful revision material.

If you have chosen to do the Research Report, choose a piece of research and practise completing the different sections of the Answer Book. Rather than doing all sections at once, you might want to do sections (a) and (b) and then read the grade-A example provided, paying particular attention to the examiner's comments. Then, choose another piece of research and complete sections (a), (b), (c) and (d). Again, read the examiner's comments for the grade-A candidate's answer. Read the grade-C candidate's answer and compare it with your own, to make sure that you are avoiding any pitfalls and are realising your full potential.

The AS specification

The aims of the OCR AS Sociology specification are:
- to give you a sound introduction to sociology regardless of whether you are only interested in gaining the AS award or whether you are aiming for the full A-level
- to develop in you an applied sociological knowledge and understanding of the concepts underpinning contemporary social processes and structures that are relevant to your social identity and your experiences of the social world
- to equip you with a theoretical awareness of how sociological perspectives explain the world you live in
- to examine how sociologists go about collecting information about the social world in which you live and whether their views on how your everyday world is organised are truthful and worthwhile
- to equip you with the necessary skills to engage in sociological debate, especially in terms of being able to interpret, apply and evaluate relevant evidence and to construct convincing sociological arguments
- to develop in you an appreciation and understanding that sociology is an interconnected academic discipline that requires you to make links between different topic areas, especially with regard to inequality and difference, and the methods of sociological enquiry

Examinable skills

There are three main examinable skills in the AS specifications, divided into two **Assessment Objectives.**

Assessment Objective 1

Assessment Objective 1 (AO1) is **knowledge and understanding**, which accounts for 54% of the AS marks on offer. After studying AS Sociology, you should be able to demonstrate knowledge and understanding of sociological concepts, methods and different types of evidence, especially empirical studies. In some units, there is a need to demonstrate some introductory knowledge of theory and especially the concepts behind it. You will need to show in a clear and effective manner how concepts, evidence and methods are interlinked, and how they relate to both social life and social problems.

It is important that your acquisition of knowledge goes beyond learning by rote. You also need to demonstrate understanding. Generally this is displayed by learning and using knowledge that is appropriate and relevant to the question set. A good way of doing this is to ask yourself the following questions:
- Do I know the main arguments in the area I am studying?
- Do I know the main sociologists who have contributed to debates in this area?
- Do I understand the concepts used by these sociologists?
- Do I know the empirical studies and data that can be used as evidence to support or undermine particular sociological arguments?

It is important to stress here that an advanced understanding of sociological theory is not required or expected. Rather, at this level, you should be 'conceptually confident', meaning that you should be able to demonstrate that you understand important concepts and are able to apply them when constructing a sociological argument. It is also a good idea to know some sociological studies because these often count as evidence in support of a particular view.

Assessment Objective 2

Assessment Objective 2 (AO2) is broken down into **AO2(a) interpretation and analysis**, which is worth 26% of the AS marks on offer, and **AO2(b) evaluation**, which is worth 20% of the AS marks.

Interpretation and analysis essentially involves showing the ability to select and analyse different types of evidence and data. In particular, it involves the ability to apply and link sociological evidence to specific sociological arguments. It also involves the ability to interpret quantitative and qualitative data, i.e. to work out what the data are saying and/or to put them into your own words. It is useful to ask yourself the following questions when working out whether you have acquired this skill:
- What knowledge in the form of studies, concepts etc. is relevant when addressing a particular debate?

- Can I distinguish between facts and opinions?
- Am I capable of identifying patterns and trends in sociological data and uncovering hidden meanings?
- Am I addressing the question throughout the response?
- Am I using the data and information that the examiners have given to me to full effect?
- Have I applied contemporary issues and debates to the question?
- What evidence in the form of sociological studies and statistical data can I use to support or criticise particular arguments?

Evaluation normally involves assessing the validity of particular sociological arguments and available evidence and data, or critically examining the reliability of the methods used to collect that evidence. The skill of evaluation is an important one and should be applied to all the material you come across during your study of the topic. It is useful to ask yourself the following questions when practising this skill:

- How many sides to the debate can be identified in this area?
- How was the evidence gathered?
- Can the evidence be checked?
- Is there any other evidence relating to this?
- Is the research relevant to contemporary society?
- Who does not agree with this view and why?
- Which evidence and arguments are most convincing and why?
- What have they got to gain from saying that?
- Are reliability, validity and representativeness taken into account?

In more practical terms, evaluation means that whenever you are introduced to a sociological perspective or study, you should find and learn at least two criticisms that have been made of it. You should also note, of course, which group or person has made these criticisms, as this is an important piece of information.

Study skills and revision strategies

Good preparation for revision actually starts the minute you begin to study sociology. One of the most important revision aids that you will have is your sociology folder, so it is important that you keep this in good order. Essentially, it should be divided into topic areas. It should contain all your class notes, handouts, notes you have made from textbooks, class and homework exercises and, of course, all your marked and returned work. If you are not by nature a neat and tidy person, you may find that you have to rewrite notes you make in class into a legible and coherent form before putting them in your folder. Be warned though, this is something you should do straight away, as even after only a few days you will have forgotten things. If you keep a good folder throughout, reading through this will form a major part of your revision. In addition, you will, of course, need to re-read the relevant parts of your textbooks. Your own work also forms an important revision resource. Go back over your essays and exam answers, read your teacher's comments, and use these to see whether you can redo any pieces that did not score particularly good marks.

You should always write down the definition of a concept when you first come across it — use a separate part of your folder for this purpose. In addition, it is useful to make a brief summary of research studies, particularly those not found in your textbook. Remember to include the title, author(s) and, most importantly, the date along with your summary of the method(s) used and the main findings. These should be kept in a section in your sociology folder, or you may wish to use a set of index cards for this purpose.

Another important aspect of revision is to practise writing answers within the appropriate time limit. Make sure you have sufficient time not only to complete all the parts of the question, but also to re-read your answer, in order to correct any silly mistakes that may have crept in while working under pressure.

Finally, you need to ensure that you have a thorough understanding of a range of appropriate concepts and studies. Again, this planned and comprehensive revision is not something that can be done the night before the exam — you should start at least a couple of weeks before the exam and revise in concentrated bursts of time. People differ in this respect, but it is seldom a good idea to spend more than 2 hours at a time on revision and, for most people, two or three stints of an hour at a time spread out over a day or two will be more productive than a 2- or 3-hour session.

The unit test/coursework

It is compulsory to take either **Sociological Research Skills** or **Research Report (Sociology)**. The unit as a whole is worth 30% of the AS marks and 15% of the full A-level.

The unit test

The unit test is worth 60 marks in total, composed of 32 marks for AO1 (knowledge and understanding), 16 marks for AO2(a) (interpretation and analysis) and 12 marks for AO2(b) (evaluation). The examination paper consists of one compulsory data–response question based on two items of data. The first item presents a limited amount of data from a piece of research (table, graph, chart, qualitative extract etc.) and the second part is an outline of a piece of proposed sociological research. The question has four parts and you are required to answer all four parts.

Do not be put off by the mark allocation. A general rule of thumb is that 1 mark is equivalent to 1 minute of writing. You should therefore spend approximately 30 minutes on parts (a), (b) and (c) and 30 minutes on part (d). Don't forget to allow yourself some time to read the items and to think about them. You should allow approximately 5 minutes to do this.

Part (a) requires you to **explain briefly** a concept such as reliability. You should be aware that there is a wide range of concepts that could be included here as well as the four key concepts. You might, for example, be required to explain concepts such as ethics, sampling and objectivity. This question is testing your knowledge and understanding and is worth 6 marks.

Part (b) requires you to use Item A and **identify two patterns**, **changes**, **trends**, **differences** etc. The marks awarded for this part are all AO2(a) (interpretation and analysis) because you are being asked to read the item and interpret what is in it. It is therefore essential that you only use the information contained in the item. Item A is a table, chart, pie diagram, graph or maybe even a piece of qualitative data. This question is worth 8 marks.

Part (c) will require you to use Item B and **identify and explain one strength and one weakness** of the research design, or **two strengths** or **two weaknesses** or **two reasons** etc. It is vital that you use the information in Item B as a starting-point for this part since marks are awarded for the ability to interpret the data in this item. There are 8 marks available for knowledge and understanding and 8 marks for interpretation and analysis, making a total of 16 marks.

Part (d) requires you to **outline and assess one sociological research method** in relation to an area of research given in the question. It is important that you focus on the given area of research throughout your answer and that you are not tempted to write a general essay on research methods. There are 18 marks available for knowledge and understanding and 12 marks for evaluation, making a total of 30 marks.

The coursework

The Research Report is worth 90 marks. It is marked out of 45 and then multiplied by two. It is worth 24 × 2 = 48 for AO1 (knowledge and understanding), 12 × 2 = 24 for AO2(a) (interpretation and analysis) and 9 × 2 = 18 for AO2(b) (evaluation).

You are required to select a piece of sociological research and write a report on it. This is an opportunity to study a piece of research that links with the work you have been doing for **Individual and Society** and **Culture and Socialisation** and which you may be able to use as evidence in the written tests for those units. If you intend to complete the full A-level, you could choose a piece of research to develop for the Personal Study at A2.

The Research Report should be written in a concise and coherent manner and you should adhere to the word length guideline of 1,000 words. You are required to write your report in an official Answer Book. Your teacher will give you a copy of this or, alternatively, you could download it from the OCR website (**www.ocr.org.uk**). Completing the report in this way may enable you to claim part of your key skills qualification.

There are four sections to be completed and they all have a prompt to tell you what you should be addressing, together with an indication of the number of words to use. It is important to stick to the word guidelines or you may find that the report becomes unbalanced. Marks for knowledge and understanding, interpretation and analysis, and evaluation will be awarded for the whole report rather than for specific sections.

Section (a)

This section requires details of the research on which you are reporting: author, title, date and the publisher/source. All these details must be provided for the report to reach the top mark level.

Section (b) (210–300 words)

In this section you should state the aims of your chosen piece of research and the research methods that were used. You should consider the methods, the sample size, the access to the sample, the sampling technique, the ethics of the research etc. Is there a research question or hypothesis? If so, what is it? You could begin to raise issues of representativeness and generalisability here. They will need to be discussed in more detail in relation to the research in section (d) but it would be appropriate to raise them here. This section gives you the opportunity to demonstrate AO1 (knowledge and understanding) skills.

Section (c) (250–300 words)

In this section you should outline the reasons why the researcher(s) chose the methodology used. You should explain why the methodology was thought to be suitable for achieving the kind of data required by the researcher(s). Was/were the researcher(s) looking for qualitative data or quantitative data or both? In this section there is an opportunity to demonstrate particularly AO2(a) (interpretation and analysis) skills.

Section (d) (350–400 words)

You are required to summarise briefly the findings of the research in this section. In doing so, you should illustrate them with extracts of the research. These extracts may be placed in an appendix that will not be included in the word count but will be considered by the examiner/moderator in relation to your ability to select appropriate material to support what you are saying about the findings. In this section, to demonstrate your AO2(b) (evaluation) skills, you should consider the extent to which the research worked well or not. You will also need to refer to the key concepts of reliability, validity, representativeness, generalisability and ethics and explain how they have affected the quality of the data collected.

Your teacher will mark your report. A sample of reports from your school or college will then be sent to an OCR moderator. You and your teacher are required to sign a front cover sheet attached to the Answer Book indicating that the work is your own.

Content Guidance

This section is intended to take you through the main areas of the OCR **Sociological Research Skills/Research Report** unit. However, it is not an exhaustive or comprehensive list of the concepts, issues and sociological studies that you could use to answer questions on this topic. Rather, it is an outline guide that should give you a good idea of the key concepts that are essential to know and some issues and sociological studies that are worth further investigation.

Basic concepts in research design

- Reliability, validity, representativeness and generalisation.
- Identifying causes and effects.
- Ethics in the research process.

Aspects of data collection

- Sampling: populations and response rates.
- Collecting primary data: quantitative and qualitative approaches; piloting, surveys, questionnaires, interviews and observation.
- Sources of secondary data: documents, libraries, official sources and the internet.

Interpreting and evaluating data

- Interpreting and evaluating quantitative data: tables and graphs.
- Interpreting and evaluating qualitative data.
- Interpreting and evaluating documents, official statistics and other secondary sources.
- Reporting research results.

The research that sociologists produce provides the evidence to support what they are saying about the social world. The OCR AS Sociological Research Skills/Research Report topic is designed to give you a good understanding of the ways in which sociologists go about collecting these data. It aims to provide you with the tools to interrogate and evaluate the research. These tools are the key concepts of **reliability**, **validity**, **representativeness** and **generalisability**. You will be expected to be able to analyse the impact that these concepts might have on the ways in which data are collected and on research designs themselves. You will be expected to know and understand why some sociologists might choose to use methods of data collection that will give them qualitative data and others choose methods that give quantitative data. There are a wide range of methods of data collection open to sociologists and you will be expected to know what these are and be able to consider the strengths and weaknesses of them and what problems might be associated with their use, including the extent to which they raise any ethical issues. Finally, you will need to be able to demonstrate your ability to interpret a range of data.

Basic concepts in research design

Central to success in this module is knowledge and understanding of four key concepts — reliability, validity, representativeness and generalisability — and the ways in which these concepts might impact upon the design of a piece of research and the findings of that research. These concepts are the tools with which, at AS, you can evaluate the effectiveness of research. You should practise applying them to research that you come across during your studies of the other two AS units, **The Individual and Society** and **Culture and Socialisation**. Using the concepts to evaluate evidence and examples will increase your evaluation marks.

Reliability

Reliability is a concept that can be applied to both the data collected and the means of data collection, i.e. the research tool or measurement procedure. It generally refers to whether the same or consistent results would be produced if the research were to be repeated by the same researcher or by other sociologists.

- Marshall (1998) identifies temporal reliability — the same result is obtained when the research is repeated or replicated at a later time.
- Marshall also identifies comparative reliability — the same result is obtained by different researchers using the same research tools or the same research is applied to similar samples taken from the same population.
- Reliability is sought by positivist sociologists who want to carry out research that is as scientific as possible — systematic, objective and logical — and who wish to generate quantitative data.
- Repeating the research may help to identify any errors in the design.
- Reliability is mainly sought by those sociologists looking for patterns and trends, those seeking to establish causes and effects and those who want to be able to generalise from one group to the whole survey population.
- Primary methods of data collection commonly used by those who want reliable data include large-scale social surveys that utilise questionnaires and structured interviews.
- Official statistics are a type of secondary data regarded as highly reliable because of the standardised way in which they are supposed to be collected.

Evaluation

- When research is repeated, the circumstances or environment may have changed. Therefore, even if the same group is being studied, the results could be different.
- On a future occasion, the people in the sample are likely to be different and the

results may therefore not be the same or even similar. For example, as Marshall notes, having once interviewed someone, a repeat interview may be contaminated by experience of the earlier interview.

- The concept of reliability is often contrasted with validity, but a reliable method can produce invalid results. For instance, the British Crime Survey is based on a highly standardised questionnaire, but its questions on crimes against the person may fail to elicit valid information about these types of crimes because victims may feel humiliated or sensitive.

Key concepts

replication; quantitative methods of data collection; positivism; validity; primary methods; secondary data; survey population

Validity

Validity is a concept that generally refers to whether research and its findings give a true picture of what is being studied, i.e. does it reflect the reality of the person/group being studied? Does the research do what it sets out to do?

- Validity is important to researchers who want to try to establish the meanings that people attach to their actions, i.e. interpretivist sociologists.
- Such researchers generally seek an in-depth insight into what a group does or thinks or feels, i.e. qualitative data.
- The primary methods of data collection commonly used by such sociologists are participant observation, non-participant observation and unstructured interviews.
- They see the secondary data obtained from expressive documents such as diaries and letters as high in validity.

Evaluation

- The results of research may be a reflection of the research device rather than the reality of what is being studied.
- People may sometimes tell the researcher what they think the researcher would like to know — this is a type of interview bias.
- The social characteristics of the researcher may influence what the people/group being studied say/tell the researcher. This is another type of interview bias.
- People in a group may change their behaviour if they think they are being watched — this is known as the Hawthorne effect.
- The researcher may interpret what he/she sees in a different way to that intended by the individuals or group being studied. In other words, there might be researcher bias.

Key concepts

in-depth information; qualitative methods of data collection; observation; unstructured interviews; Interpretivist sociology; interview bias; researcher bias; Hawthorne effect

NB Don't confuse the concepts of reliability and validity. One way to do this is to avoid linking them together when you write your answers.

Representativeness

This concept generally means that the group being studied is typical of the survey population. The individual sampling unit — the individual or group being researched — reflects the characteristics of the research population as a whole in terms of social class, age, gender, ethnicity etc. This concept is of particular importance to sociologists who want to do research from which they can then make generalisations.

Evaluation

- To obtain respondents who are typical of the population being studied, the sampling method must be purposive. Sampling methods such as random, stratified and quota sampling are all purposive methods.
- Where a researcher has chosen an opportunity sample, that is, selected individuals or groups who just happen to be available, it would be unsafe to make any claim that the results reflected the views of the total population being studied.
- Sampling techniques, such as snowball or volunteer sampling, do not lend themselves to obtaining a representative sample. However, sociologists who use these methods may not be seeking a representative sample. For instance, research on house-husbands will not generally claim to be representative of all men in live-in relationships with women.

Key concepts

typicality; sample size; sampling frame; sampling unit; sampling technique

Generalisability

This concept generally refers to the ability to make claims about a survey population based on a sample. Its success depends upon a number of factors such as:
- the size of the sample
- the sampling method used, i.e. whether it is purposive or not
- the extent to which it could be claimed that the sample units are typical of the population and reflect its social characteristics

Evaluation

- Is it possible to say something about the whole population being studied based on the sample actually studied? Would it be reasonable to claim that all young women of 20–25 in London have a particular view about marriage and motherhood, based on research carried out on a random stratified sample from across the city?
- Is it possible to make a claim about a population that has not been studied? For example, would it be possible to say something about the views of young women across Britain on marriage and motherhood based on research undertaken on a random stratified sample of London women?

– The social characteristics of a sample might reflect those of the total population, but it does not mean that it is necessarily possible to make statements about the broader population based on the sample studied.

Key concepts

representativeness; sample size; typicality

Identifying causes and effects

Two ways of viewing the world, positivism and interpretivism, have dominated sociology for many years, although there have been recent challenges to these. At AS you should have an awareness of these two traditions and how they may affect the collection of data. It is not necessary to know them in detail or to be able to mount a detailed theoretical critique of them. This can be left until the full A-level if you decide to complete that. You should also have some understanding of some challenges to these traditional ways of viewing the world from perspectives such as feminism.

How does positivism view the social world?

- Society — the social world — can be studied in an objective way.
- Social facts exist which can be studied in the same or similar ways to the natural world.
- Society exists outside of the individuals who comprise it.
- Individuals are subject to external social forces, such as value consensus, social class, patriarchy etc., and consequently individual and social behaviour is shaped and constrained by the social organisation or social structure of society.
- Society can be studied in a logical, systematic way using the methods of the natural sciences, i.e. research questions/hypotheses can be tested using methods thought to be scientific in that they are assumed to be objective and value free, such as survey questionnaires, structured interviews, experiments and official statistics.
- Positivists seek to collect quantitative data in order to establish cause and effect relationships between social phenomena, such as social behaviour, and aspects of social structure, such as social class.
- Such social relationships are seen to constitute social laws that underpin all human action.

The characteristics of quantitative data

- Data that can be expressed in a numerical form.
- They are often presented in the form of graphs, tables and bar charts.
- Such data allow sociologists to make comparisons over time.
- Such data allow sociologists to identify patterns and trends.
- They underpin positivist attempts to try to establish correlations between two or more variables.

- Quantitative data are easily available from official sources such as Social Trends or **www.statistics.gov.uk**.

Evaluation

- Science is itself unscientific because to be objective and value free in the social world is seen by many as problematic.
- Humans have free will and are not subject to the same laws as scientific phenomena, i.e. they cannot be studied scientifically.
- Science is over-deterministic in that it neglects the human capacity to change patterns of behaviour.
- Links between two variables do not necessarily mean they are related in terms of cause and effect. For example, women are now in a position to pursue a career and divorce has become easier to obtain but, while these two facts may be linked, it is not possible to argue that one has necessarily caused the other.
- Quantitative data may tell us more about the groups involved in their collection than the social phenomena they are meant to describe. They may tell us more about the sociologist's version of reality.
- Quantitative data are seen to be high in reliability but they can be low in validity. For example, crime statistics can be collected over and over again but they tell us about crimes reported rather than the reality of the amount and extent of crime in society.
- Many sociologists today combine theoretical perspectives in that they believe social behaviour to be the result of a combination of choice and structural influences. For instance, educational success may be held back by factors beyond our control, such as our social class, gender and/or ethnicity, but some working-class children defy the odds and succeed or redefine success to fit their own experience.
- Sociologists today tend to use whatever method is best — usually a variety of methods (see triangulation) is adopted in order to generate quantitative data supported by qualitative information. For example, questionnaire survey data may be backed up by unstructured interviews.

Key concepts

positivism; quantitative methods of data collection; cause and effect; social laws; social structure; reliability; validity

How does interpretivism view the social world?

- Human beings differ from the objects of scientific research — animals, plants, chemicals — in that they have consciousness.
- Human behaviour is not determined by social laws and is not predictable because humans can exercise choice and make decisions to pursue alternative courses of action.
- Individuals are active, not passive. They create their own destinies rather than having them shaped by social structures.
- The social world is socially constructed in that it is the product of shared inter-action and the meanings or interpretations that humans use to make sense of that interaction.

- The role of sociologists is to uncover these shared interpretations.
- Sociological research should endeavour to get inside people's heads and experience the world from their point of view. This is empathetic understanding or 'verstehen'.
- Interpretivists stress the importance of primary methods such as unstructured interviews and observation.
- Secondary forms of data approved of by interpretivists include personal documents such as diaries and letters, historical documents and mass media reports.
- Science, objectivity and reliability are less important than the validity that characterises the qualitative data gathered by interpretivist methods.

The characteristics of qualitative data

- Data that can be expressed in words, for example in the form of conversational analysis, interview transcripts, ethnographic descriptions, diary entries.
- Such data give an insight into the feelings, opinions and thoughts of those researched.
- Qualitative data provide an in-depth account of the meanings that individuals and groups attach to their lives and the social world in which they live.
- Qualitative data allow those being studied to speak for themselves.
- They focus on the interactions of the researched with each other and with others.
- They allow research to be undertaken in the respondents' own environment.

Evaluation

- Interpretivism is often accused by positivists of being too subjective.
- Individuals only exercise agency (choices) within constraints (social structures).
- Qualitative data are often the product of the interpretations of the researchers, because they select the data they feel are important and this may reflect their prejudices.
- Many sociologists today combine theoretical perspectives, in that they believe social behaviour to be the result of a combination of choice and structural influences. For example, educational success may be held back by factors beyond our control, such as our social class, gender and/or ethnicity, but some working-class children defy the odds and succeed or redefine success to fit their own experience.
- Sociologists today tend to use whatever method is best. Usually a variety of methods (see triangulation) is adopted in order to generate quantitative data supported by qualitative information. For example, questionnaire survey data may be backed up by unstructured interviews.

Key concepts

validity; subjectivity; verstehen; interpretations; meanings; social construction; empathetic understanding; interaction; agency, ethnographic; qualitative data; conversational analysis; triangulation

Ethics in the research process

Sociologists frequently seek information of a personal, sensitive or even illegal nature. The acquisition of such information may raise ethical issues, i.e. issues that have a moral implication for either the respondents or the researcher. The British Sociological Association has produced guidelines on the ethics of doing research, but some sociologists, such as those who choose to do covert observation, would argue that the very nature of their research is such that they cannot entirely adhere to those guidelines. Feminists have tried to break down the hierarchy between the researcher and the researched, arguing that the power relationship is itself unethical and can impede the development of trust between the two.

Respondents (the researched) have the right:
- to anonymity and privacy
- to confidentiality
- not to be placed in physical harm or danger of any sort
- to be asked for their informed consent
- to have sensitive issues dealt with sensitively

The researchers should not:
- place themselves in danger
- condone illegal activities
- be dishonest with those they are researching

Evaluation

- Research in some areas might identify a person by his/her position, e.g. the head-teacher of a school.
- In the past, researchers have written up their research in such a way as to ignore the right to privacy on behalf of their respondents, an example being research in schools by Hargreaves.
- Abiding by the law may risk the researcher's access to a criminal or deviant group or undermine their trust in the researcher. Both Dick Hobbs and Howard Parker engaged in illegal activities in order to maintain their position with petty criminals and juvenile delinquents respectively.
- Being honest may lead to the Hawthorne effect.
- There are many examples of researchers who have not reported illegal activities by their respondents to the police, for example, Hobbs and James Patrick.
- Even where informed consent is sought, the respondents may not fully understand what is being asked for in terms of the publication of their activities.
- Research carried out with respondents who see themselves as 'friends' of the researcher could leave them feeling let down when the research is finished and the contact is reduced or lost completely. For example, the first-time mothers whom Oakley worked with in *From Here to Maternity* lost their 'friend' and 'confidant'.
- Giving the respondents the opportunity to read what has been written about them

is not always straightforward. For instance, Paul Willis's 'lads' said they could understand the direct quotes from themselves that he had included, but the rest made no sense.

– Researchers who use ethnographic methods may find it difficult or even impossible to inform the people/group whom they are researching that they are doing research because of the possibility of the Hawthorne effect.

– It may be impossible to break down the power relationships that are contained in researcher–researched relationships.

Key concepts

privacy; confidentiality; informed consent; illegal activities; Hawthorne effect

Aspects of data collection

- Primary data collection refers to data that sociologists have collected for themselves, or with the help of others working with them.
- Secondary data collection refers to data that sociologists may choose to use, or have to use, that have been collected by others.
- Whether the data collected are primary or secondary, they might be qualitative or quantitative.

Practical and theoretical constraints

The decision to carry out sociological research is not a straightforward process and depends upon a range of practical and theoretical factors with regard to the choice of topic to research and methods used.

Practical constraints

- The source of funding — some research may be for purely academic purposes and consequently funded by the Economic and Social Research Council and universities, while other types may be funded by business to promote particular interests, such as research into worker motivation.
- The values that underpin social science research are not always shaped by neutral scientific detachment but may seek to support particular political and social interests.
- The amount of monies available will shape the methodological tools used by researchers. A lack of substantial funds may mean reliance on cheaper methods, such as questionnaires, because of the costs of long-term observation and the training of interviewers.
- The length of time the researchers have available to them — if the researchers

have a couple of years as well as the funding, they may elect to undertake a longitudinal survey or an observation study.

- Whether the research is to be undertaken by a sole researcher or team of researchers.
- Some research is the outcome of what is fashionable at the time in sociology. Note the glut of education studies, especially by feminist and interactionist sociologists, in the 1960s and 1970s.
- Access to the group or individuals to be studied is crucial, i.e. some social groups have the power to resist sociological investigation — note the lack of sociological studies of private education compared with comprehensive schools.
- The social characteristics of the researcher or research team are very important. Social class, gender, age, ethnicity, accents, dress, personality etc. are all factors which may impact positively or negatively on research design. For example, a team of researchers aged 40 and above investigating the attitudes of teenagers will need to think about how they can avoid their age and perceived authority undermining the validity of their research data.
- The ethical nature of the proposed research is important. For example, the sociological investigation into the relationship between media content and children's behaviour is difficult to pursue in any depth because exposing children to violent images may have an effect of some sort.
- All sociological researchers need to be aware of the British Sociological Association's guidelines.

Theoretical constraints

- The theoretical perspective of the sociologists, that is the way in which they understand the social world, may affect both their hypothesis/research questions and their chosen research method. For instance, a feminist researcher may have different priorities and interests when compared with a Marxist or New Right sociologist.
- Similarly, the values of the researchers may impact on their research focus. Do they see the social world as characterised by consensus or conflict; do they want to right wrongs and social injustice; are they believers in equal opportunities?
- Does the researcher wish to demonstrate cause and effect from the data or merely describe aspects of the social world?
- Is the researcher trying to understand how the researched experience their world in terms of the meanings and motives they attach to actions?
- Textbooks often state that whether a sociologist is positivist or interpretivist will affect how research is carried out. For example, positivist research into teenage mothers will supposedly focus on the extent of the 'problem' and identifying their social characteristics, whereas interpretivists are supposedly more interested in how teenage mothers feel about their situation.

Evaluation

- The positivist versus interpretivist debate is overstated because most sociological research uses whatever method works best. In many research situations, this usually involves a combination of quantitative and qualitative methods — see 'Triangulation', on pp. 34–35.

Key concepts

social characteristics; consensus; conflict; meanings and motives

Sampling: populations and response rates

The survey population

- The survey or research population refers to all the people relevant to the area being studied — a study being done on AS sociology students in Birmingham means that the target or survey population is AS sociology students in Birmingham.
- The survey population could be the total population of Britain as is the case of the 10-yearly census.
- Generally, sociologists do not have the resources to target the whole of the British population. Consequently they tend to focus on smaller and more manageable social groups that share common social characteristics, e.g. AS students in Birmingham.

Sampling

- Sampling techniques are the methods whereby a sociologist selects a small group from the survey population.
- Sampling units are the groups or individuals selected from the wider survey population for study — it could be an individual, a couple, a household or a group.
- The technique or method of selection may vary depending on what the sociologists want to do with their findings. If they are hoping to generalise from their research findings to the wider group, they will need to ensure that their sample units are large enough and typical of the population being studied.
- For some sociologists a sample representative of the complete survey population is not an issue because they only want to demonstrate evidence of a particular activity in the form of a case study. For example, a sample of men who act as house-husbands would not be representative of husbands as a whole but would demonstrate that some men do take on the role.
- A sampling frame is a list of all or most of the units to be researched, such as the electoral register, the telephone directory, membership lists of organisations and school registers.
- Maps have often been used by sociologists in the absence of a conventional sampling frame. A map of a town or city can be divided into smaller areas, such as electoral districts, neighbourhoods and streets, and all households in those areas targeted.

- Care needs to be taken with using electoral rolls or registers (lists of households) as they may be incomplete because people are avoiding paying council tax, people may have died or moved away, the homeless are excluded and children aged 17 and under are not included.
- A telephone directory obviously excludes those who do not have telephones and ex-directory numbers. Therefore, a sociological investigation into people's perceptions of privacy might run into problems using a telephone directory as the sampling frame.
- Sometimes sampling frames are inaccessible because of ethical issues such as privacy and confidentiality. For example, a doctor is unlikely to agree to allow students to access his/her patients' files.
- Sampling frames are not objective or neutral sources of information — they reflect the interests and prejudices of the people who make them up. For example, school registers from a comprehensive school in a leafy suburb are likely to contain an over-proportionate number of middle-class white pupils.
- There are unlikely to be sampling frames of deviant or criminal groups available.

Sampling techniques

There is a variety of random and non-random sampling techniques available to sociologists. Random sampling is regarded as both objective and scientific because everybody in the survey population has an equal chance or probability of being selected. The aim of this type of sample is to exclude the possibility of bias that potentially infects those non-random sampling methods that involve some degree of selection. It is also thought that randomly generated samples are more likely to be representative or typical of the survey population being studied if particular random sampling techniques are used that mean generalisations to the whole of the survey population are possible.

Random or probability sampling
- **Simple random sampling** involves drawing X number of names from a list or, more frequently, programming a computer to generate names randomly.
- **Systematic random sampling** involves the selection of every nth name from a sampling frame.
- **Stratified random sampling** involves the survey population being divided up according to the variables that the researcher wishes to include. The researcher may wish to distinguish between working-class and middle-class respondents, between different age groups, or between men and women. Every nth name will then be selected from the appropriate variable list, e.g. by a computer so that the final sample reflects the social characteristics of the survey population.
- **Cluster random sampling** normally involves using a map as a sampling frame, randomly selecting neighbourhoods or streets and researching all households in those areas.
- **Multi-stage random sampling** involves randomly selecting particular types of people, such as occupational groups, or areas from a sampling frame or map, and randomly selecting subsamples for comparison, e.g. doctors, solicitors or particular roads and streets.

- Despite the fact that every social group in the survey population has an equal chance of being picked, systematic sampling can lead to a skewed and therefore biased sample.
- Stratified sampling is time-consuming.
- A sample is unlikely to reflect completely the group from which it is drawn, because there will be sampling errors.
- It is difficult, if not impossible, to identify accurately everyone in the population being studied.

Non-random sampling

- **Quota sampling** involves the researcher deciding how many people should be in each category of the population he/she is studying and then personally selecting them.
- **Snowball sampling** involves the researcher asking already identified respondents to be put in touch with others the respondents know who 'fit' the researcher's criteria. This is often used to gain access to members of deviant or criminal groups for example, who cannot be approached 'officially', or who the researcher would not otherwise be able to reach.
- **Volunteer sampling** involves the researcher seeking potential respondents by advertising.
- **Opportunistic sampling** involves the researcher asking those respondents who just happen to be about and who 'fit' the researcher's criteria.

Evaluation

- Non-random sampling is useful when there is no sampling frame.
- Non-random techniques are useful if a particular type of sampling unit or respondent is required.
- Samples generated by these techniques are likely to be very similar to each other, although this will not matter for some research because the researcher is attempting to access a specific group. For example, Sharpe used snowball sampling in *Double Identity* to reach working mothers.

Key concepts

social survey; survey population; sample; sampling frame; sampling unit; random sampling; non-random sampling; representativeness; generalisations; skewed sample; typicality; probability; variables

Operationalisation

Once a sociologist decides upon a research question/hypothesis, it needs to be developed and broken down into a set of components or indicators that can be observed and measured. For example, if 'fear of crime' is the central research focus, the researcher needs to define the term precisely and especially in a way that is shared by a potential survey population. Once a definition is agreed upon, the researcher needs to identify components of 'fear of crime' that can be turned into questions suitable for a questionnaire/interview schedule, categories of behaviour that can be recorded on an observation schedule, categories of media representation that can be recorded on a content analysis schedule etc. Moreover, the researcher needs to operationalise aspects of the research population. This means the researcher needs to decide on the social characteristics of the sample and consequently the means he/she (e.g. factual questions in a survey) by which he/she might ensure he/she is measuring differences in attitude or behaviour on the basis of these characteristics.

- Research design in the form of questionnaires and observation/content analysis schedules is a crucial element of operationalisation.
- It is important that questions or categories used in observation/content analysis schedules do not reflect the researcher's own values, interpretations and prejudices.
- It is important that questions and categories do not 'force' respondents into making artificial responses. Loaded (emotional, subjective) questions, e.g. 'Are you a racist?', and leading questions, e.g. 'Don't you think sex before marriage is disgusting?', should be avoided.

Evaluation

- Interpretivists argue that a value-free type of research is impossible, that is, sociologists always end up imposing their view of reality on respondents through questions etc.
- They also argue that most research methods, with the exception of ethnographic methods, are artificial in that people do not normally experience these on an everyday basis and are therefore likely to react in artificial ways to them.
- All research is based on interaction between researcher and researched and such interaction impacts on both the reliability and validity of the research process and findings — see 'Interview effect' on p. 28.
- Operationalisation is regarded as unreliable by interpretivists because different sociologists may operationalise and measure hypotheses and research questions in quite different ways.

Key concepts

operationalisation; hypothesis; ethnographic methods

Collecting primary data

- Primary data are any data that sociologists have collected through methods such as sample surveys (using questionnaires and/or structured interviews) and unstructured interviews and observation.
- The collection of primary data may generate quantitative or qualitative data.

Quantitative approaches

There are a number of methods that can be used to collect quantitative data.

Social or sample surveys

- Social or sample surveys are methods of research often used by positivists that enable the researcher to gain large quantities of data from a representative sample of the survey population.
- The research device/tool is often a questionnaire, although structured interviews can also be used.
- Surveys can be snapshot (a group is studied at a particular period in time) or longitudinal (a group is studied over a period of years). Parker's research on drug use took 5 years whilst Douglas's study of child-rearing and parental interest in education took place over decades.

Questionnaires

- These may be administered in a number of ways such as by post/mail, through magazines and newspapers, by hand, by the internet and/or email.
- Respondents complete them for themselves. If a questionnaire is completed by a researcher, it is an interview schedule, not a questionnaire.
- Questionnaires are supposedly favoured by positivists because they are regarded as being systematic, objective and scientific.
- Questionnaires, especially those that use closed questions, are regarded as being high in reliability because they can be replicated easily by other sociologists to obtain similar results.
- Questions are standardised and may include open and closed questions or a combination of the two.
- Questionnaires can be pre-coded for ease of statistical analysis.
- Large amounts of quantitative data as well as qualitative data can be collected from open questions.
- The statistical data gathered can be tabulated and used as the basis of comparative analysis.

Evaluation

- Critics suggest that questionnaires result in the imposition of the sociologist's view of the world, in that the questions asked are the questions the sociologist has decided are important rather than the respondent.
- Questionnaires and structured interview schedules are social constructs. They reflect the values, interests and priorities of the researcher, which might be quite different from those held by the survey population.
- Respondents are often not able to elaborate on their feelings and emotions.
- Response rates are notoriously low for postal questionnaires.
- If the questionnaire is a postal one, the researcher can never be sure that the right person has completed it.
- If the questionnaires are given out by hand, the research may still be negatively influenced by interviewer bias since the respondents know to whom they are responding.
- If open questions have been used, there is sometimes a difficulty in analysing the responses in any meaningful way.
- There is the danger that the researcher may misinterpret any information gathered.

Response rates
- The extent to which the sample chosen is effective will depend on the response rate of the respondents selected.
- Postal questionnaires have a very low rate of return, the average being about 30%; anything over 50% is very good.
- Those who receive postal questionnaires may simply not return them. Face-to-face questionnaires and interviews may be more appropriate in order to reduce the non-response rate and refusals.
- Those returning postal questionnaires are a self-selected group who may not be typical of the survey population.
- Variations in response rates are likely to have a negative effect on the research findings and therefore on the ability of the researcher to generalise from the sample to the total survey population — a poor response rate will probably mean that the sample is unrepresentative.

Pilot studies or surveys
- These are done prior to a main study in order to check the questionnaire and the sampling technique.
- Although pilot studies can be used with any method of data collection, they are most commonly used with social surveys.
- Piloting or trialling can save time and money if there is a problem with the research device (questionnaire, interview schedule etc.).
- A questionnaire can be trialled in terms of its effectiveness so that questions that do not work or that are unclear can be reworded.
- Ease of access to the sample can be checked.
- The appropriateness of the sample can be checked.
- The sampling technique can be checked; for instance, the response rate can be estimated.

Structured interviews
- These are another means of collecting quantitative data.
- The researcher asks the questions face-to-face and all respondents are asked the same questions in the same order.
- If there is a team of interviewers, they will be trained in order that there is standardisation of practice.
- With some structured interviews there is the option for the interviewer to clarify any misunderstanding by the respondents, although it should be noted that once this happens the interview is moving away from the strictly structured interview.
- Such interviews can be carried out in the interviewee's home, which might increase trust on the part of the respondent, leading to more valid responses in terms of honesty etc.
- Structured interviews tend to have a better response rate than postal question-naires.
- Standardised questions mean that comparisons can be made.

Evaluation
  – Interviews are more expensive than questionnaires because they involve employing and training people to conduct the interviews in a standardised fashion.
  – Sample sizes for interviews tend to be smaller for practical reasons.

Interview effect

All interviews are interactions. When people interact, they use a set of meanings or interpretations to make sense of the situation they are in and to work out how they should respond to the other people involved in the interaction. This may impact upon the reliability of the research process and the validity of the research findings in the following ways:

- The subjects of the research may feel threatened by the status of the interviewer. For example, the age, social class, gender, ethnicity and even the sexuality of the researcher may be interpreted as sufficiently different to undermine the cooperation of the research subject and therefore the validity of the data.
- Children may interpret adult interviewers as authoritative. Consequently they may be unwilling to discuss aspects of their experience or feelings that they think might get them into trouble.
- Research subjects may interpret factors such as dress and accent as indicators of status so interviewers have to think very carefully about the presentation of their status — it must be as neutral as possible.
- Interviewers have to be careful that their tone of voice, facial expression, body language etc. does not 'lead' respondents into giving the answer the research subjects think the researcher wants.
- Interviewers have to avoid the 'social desirability' effect — respondents may want the researcher to approve of them and engage in 'yea-saying', i.e. agreeing with the researcher regardless, or fictionalising or exaggerating aspects of their experience and attitudes having worked out what the researcher is looking for.
- The environment in which the research is conducted must not be threatening — it would not be a good idea to interview a pupil in the headteacher's study.

Key concepts

sample surveys; quantitative; qualitative; longitudinal; standardisation; comparative analysis; social construct; interview bias or effect; non-response rate; pilot study; reliability; validity

Qualitative approaches

- These are used by sociologists who are seeking data that provide an in-depth look into the world of those being researched.
- Qualitative methods include semi-structured and unstructured interviews and observation.

Semi-structured interviews

- These usually have an interview schedule made up of predetermined topic areas.

- Within those areas the interviewer has some flexibility to ask a range of questions in order to obtain the information required.
- Some of the questions may be standardised so that some basic information about each respondent can be gathered.

Unstructured interviews

- This type of interview gives the interviewer greatest freedom to explore an area with a respondent.
- Unstructured interviews are often used by feminists who argue that they allow for the greatest possible breakdown of the hierarchical relationship that exists between researcher and researched.
- Although there is usually some kind of list of topic areas to be covered, the interviewer is given freedom to allow the interview to follow its own course.
- These types of interview are usually conducted in a place convenient to the interviewee, such as at home, in a local pub or café or in a park, so that the interviewee feels as relaxed and comfortable as possible.
- Such interviews allow the development of a rapport between interviewer and interviewee and a relationship of trust, which can then increase the extent and depth of information that can be obtained.
- Such interviews are well suited to sensitive topic areas.
- The data from such interviews are thought to be high in validity.
- Such interviews enable researchers to uncover information that they did not know they wanted.

Evaluation

- Like structured interviews, unstructured interviews are subject to interviewer bias, although the special relationship between the interviewer and interviewee is likely to reduce its impact upon the research findings.
- Positivist sociologists claim unstructured interviews are too subjective, because the interviewer is not detached enough from the interviewee and consequently this undermines the objectivity of the research.
- If more than one interviewer is involved, interpretation of information becomes more problematic.
- It is difficult for another researcher to repeat the research and obtain the same results, so there is some claim that such research is low in reliability.
- Recording interviews is problematic. Tape-recording ensures all the data are available for analysis but may be inappropriate in some circumstances, whereas taking notes may act as a barrier between the researcher and the researched.
- Some sociologists, including some feminists, have recently returned to using group interviews/focus groups, originally used by Merton in the 1940s, as a means of obtaining detailed information on very specific areas.

Key concepts

validity; rapport; trust; non-hierarchical relationship; focus interviews; group interviews; objectivity

Observation

- Observation may be done by participating in the activities of a group in either a covert (hidden) or overt (open) manner or by being a non-participant, again either in a covert or overt way.
- The decision as to which type of observation to adopt will depend on the group being researched as well as the ethics of the researcher.
- This type of research is particularly favoured by interpretivists who stress the need for ethnographic research (the researching of groups in their natural environments).
- Interpretivists aim to 'get inside the heads' of those they are researching, because in order to understand human behaviour, we need to understand how people interpret the social worlds around them.
- Weber's concept of 'verstehen' is important. He believed sociologists should try to understand and empathise with people before attempting to interpret their actions.
- Observation is seen to produce extremely valid data, especially if people are not aware that the researcher is present or sufficient time has elapsed since the entry of the observer that his/her presence is taken for granted.
- Observation often uncovers behaviour — especially deviant, criminal and unethical behaviour — that is unlikely to be admitted by respondents when filling in a questionnaire or participating in a one-off structured interview.
- There is often a gap between what people say and what they actually do, and observation can focus on this. For example, Cicourel found police officers in the USA acting in a racist fashion towards black people, despite their insistence that they treated everybody equally.

Participant observation

- This type of observation requires the researcher to enter a group, become accepted as a member, join in the activities of the group and then eventually leave.
- It enables the researcher to see people in their natural environment, without disturbing them too much.
- There are two types of participant observation, covert and overt; the decision as to which to use will sometimes depend on the group and the extent to which it will allow a 'stranger' in.
- Data from participant and non-participant observation are usually qualitative, but the use of a matrix or observation schedule can lead to some quality quantitative data.

Non-participant observation

- The researcher takes a role that enables the researcher to observe a group without participating in the activities of the group.
- Non-participant observation may be covert, for instance through one-way mirrors, although this method is more likely to be used by psychologists.
- An example of overt non-participation could be the observations of teacher–pupil interactions carried out by sociologists such as Hargreaves, Willis and Ball.
- Overt non participant observation allows the researcher to be more honest with the group that is being researched and provides the sociologist with a reason for not participating in illegal activities.

- Often an observation schedule or matrix is used to record quantitative data, e.g. by counting particular interactions or types of behaviour.

Covert participant observation

- This type of observation involves the researcher joining the group undercover and merging into the group identity by adopting its dress code, behavioural patterns etc.
- This is problematic since it requires the researcher to deceive the researched and possibly also puts the researcher in danger.
- Covert observation is less likely than other methods to interfere with or change the natural behaviour of the group being researched.
- The study of some groups, street gangs, football hooligans and the police is only really possible by covert participant observation.
- Some research would be impossible if the researcher was completely honest about what he/she was doing. Consequently, some researchers only tell half a story to some of the members of the group. For example, Whyte, Pryce and Hobbs all did this to give themselves a way into a group without deceiving its members completely.

Overt participant observation

- The researcher tells the group, or some of the people in the group, what he/she is doing.
- Behaviour is observed in its natural setting.
- This method overcomes the problem of deceit.

Evaluation

- Observation is criticised for its lack of reliability because the observation relationship depends on the success of particular individuals in establishing covert/overt relationships with the group being studied. This is extremely difficult to replicate.
- Access is sometimes difficult, particularly to closed groups such as travellers. Both Okely and Martin had to work hard to earn the trust of the travellers whom they researched.
- The social characteristics of sociologists, for example their gender, age and/or ethnicity, will in some circumstances preclude the use of this method.
- The Hawthorne effect may occur — people's behaviour may be changed by the presence of the researcher.
- Covert observation may lead to the researcher 'going native', i.e. becoming so much a part of the group that he/she is no longer able to stand back and make any objective interpretation of what is taking place.
- Recording data is problematic. It is not usually possible to tape-record or write field notes at the time, so researchers tend to rely on memory, which may be subjectively over-selective in support of a hypothesis, theory or political position.
- One difficulty is how to become sufficiently involved, as the group may be suspicious of the researcher's motives and resist the active involvement of the researcher.

Key concepts

covert observation; overt observation; participant observation; non-participant observation; verstehen; empathy; ethnographic

Sources of secondary data

- Secondary data refer to any data that sociologists have used which they did not collect for themselves.
- Such data include official statistics; personal or expressive documents such as diaries, letters, photographs, paintings and novels; public or official documents such as government reports and reports of other organisations such as companies; historical documents; mass media reports such as television, newspapers, magazines, the radio and the internet.
- The research of other sociologists and government bodies is often used as a starting-point for researchers or as a point of comparison or reference.
- Much of this material will be available through local and national libraries.

Personal documents

- Personal documents are usually diaries, letters and other expressive documents.
- They can provide a sociologist with a rich source of qualitative data.
- They are often used to supplement secondary data that is quantitative, such as official statistics. For instance, a diary or letters may be used to give some meaning to public data on size of families, numbers of children and employment patterns.
- They may also be used where no other source of data exists, such as the now famous research by Thomas and Znaniecki on Polish peasants in Europe and America which used diaries, letters and newspaper articles. More recently, Valerie Hey used schoolgirls' notes as one method of researching friendships.

Public documents

- Public documents include government reports, reports of companies and reports from trade unions.
- They often provide a basic picture upon which further research can be undertaken.

Evaluation

- The authenticity of documents, particularly historical documents, is often questioned. Are they genuine or not? Were they written by the person whom it is claimed wrote them?
- Is the material as accurate a portrayal of the events or issues as possible, or was it written to give a selective, prejudiced, partial and therefore biased view of some historical event? For example, the memoirs and letters of politicians may lack objectivity.
- Could the document(s) be said to be typical of material on the particular subject?
- Are the authors representative of the social group to which they belong?
- To what extent is the meaning of the contents of the document(s) clear or is it open to interpretation?
- Many expressive/personal documents provide detailed information not obtainable elsewhere and increase the insights of researchers.

Official statistics

- These are statistics produced by government departments.
- They cover all aspects of social life, such as crime, health, family life and education, and can be accessed via the internet or publications such as *Social Trends*.
- The most commonly available source of official statistics are those from the census; this mass survey, last conducted in 2001, is carried out every tenth year on the whole population.
- Other government surveys include the General Household Survey, the Family Expenditure Survey and the Labour Force Survey.
- Official statistics are cheap to access, cover a variety of sociologically relevant topics and are easily available.
- They have comparative value — past statistics can be compared with contemporary statistics to assess the success or failure of social policies.

Evaluation

- Official statistics may not present a complete picture — for example, crime statistics only cover reported crime.
- They may be used to put a particular political slant on an issue and consequently may be biased. For example, governments frequently change the ways in which unemployment statistics are collected in order to make the problem look better than it actually is.
- Statistics are socially constructed, meaning that they tell us more about the priorities and interests of the people who collect them than about the social phenomena they are supposed to describe.
- Official statistics are not collected for sociological purposes so their usefulness may be limited. Government officials may use different definitions, means of measurement and interpretations to those acceptable to sociologists.

NB *It is worth spending some time looking at the numerical data in* Social Trends *since there is usually a written commentary alongside the tables, charts and diagrams which points out trends and patterns. You will need to do this in part (b) of the written paper. In addition, the ability to do this for yourself is a synoptic skill and should be practised throughout your studies. The data in the most recent volume of* Social Trends *will be up to date and you will be able to use them in other AS units such as* **The Family** *option in the* **Culture and Socialisation** *unit.*

Key concepts

secondary data; official government statistics; expressive documents (diaries, letters etc.); media reports; historical documents; authenticity; social construction

Content analysis

- Content analysis involves the detailed analysis of a form of the media, such as television advertising, women's magazines, newspapers and children's readers.
- It requires the researcher to identify a set of categories that operationalise a

research question or hypothesis in order to 'count' the number of times such categories occur.

- It results in quantitative data from a systematic analysis of qualitative material and can be used as a comparative tool. For example, Best repeated Lobban's study of children's books in order to assess progress over 20 years.
- Some types of content analysis involve a qualitative analysis of language, headlines, photographs etc., e.g. the Glasgow University Media Group's analysis of news.
- Content analysis is used by positivists and interpretivist sociologists alike.
- It is generally regarded as a cheap and easily accessible means of research because mass media reports are readily available and there is no need to gather a representative sample audience for questionnaire or interview purposes.

Evaluation

- The reliability of content analysis has been questioned because the categories are determined by the researcher — different researchers may interpret such categories in different ways in terms of importance, impact on the audience and so on.
- It can be a time-consuming method.
- The validity of research findings produced by content analysis has been questioned because data are selected according to the interpretations of the researcher; what one sociologist may see as a negative representation of women may be seen by another as a neutral or positive representation.
- It is often assumed by sociologists using content analysis that media representations, content etc. have some effect upon the audience, but this has never been convincingly proved.

The internet

Throughout your studies you should make use of the internet. However, you need to use it with caution since there are so many sites that could occupy hours of your time to no real purpose. A useful starting-point is an item in *Sociology Review* entitled 'Eyes on the net'. A fairly recent trend is for research to be carried out over the internet. These projects tend to be mostly questionnaire-based, but some are interview-based, and there has been some ethnographic research based on specific communities in cyberspace, e.g. entering chat-rooms and 'observing' cyber-interaction.

Evaluation

- It is important to employ a healthy scepticism towards the content of websites. If you use websites, try and make sure you are using those recommended by your teacher, *Sociology Review* and sociological organisations.
- Research using the net means that the sample will be a self-selected group with the attendant problems of bias, although 'interviewer bias' may well be reduced.

Triangulation

- Most contemporary sociological research has moved away from the simplistic division of positivism and interpretivism. In fact, some sociologists argue that such a division was largely the product of the imagination of textbook writers.

- The reality is that sociologists often use more than one method when doing research in order to verify the results they obtain. This is known as triangulation.
- It is common to find that sociologists use methods of data collection that provide them with both quantitative and qualitative data. For instance, a large-scale social survey may be backed up by carrying out a number of unstructured interviews, or systematic non-participant observation might provide material for questionnaires or interviews. Barker's research on the Moonies and Willis's study of the 'lads' use forms of triangulation.
- The reliability of methods and the validity of the findings they generate can be cross-checked by the use of a second or third method and vice versa.

Evaluation

- Do not make the mistake of seeing triangulation as a method — it is an approach to collecting data that uses two or three methods.
- Triangulation should not be confused with methodological pluralism, which is a concept dealt with at A2.

Interpreting and evaluating data

In order to be successful in this unit you must be able to read and interpret data. You must be able to identify patterns and trends and be able to compare one piece of data with another. You should be able to comment on the strengths and weaknesses of research designs.

Quantitative data

Quantitative data are usually presented in the form of tables, graphs, charts and diagrams, although it is possible that there will be a written commentary as is the case in *Social Trends*. In order to read and evaluate charts, tables and graphs effectively, you need to approach them in a systematic and logical manner.

- Read the title — it will tell you what the data is about.
- Find the source — this will give you some idea about the reliability and general status of the data, e.g. are they from a government department?
- The date they were collected/published should give you some indication of how up to date the information is.
- Read any supplementary notes that are included in order to elaborate on the data.
- Check what the axes on graphs represent.
- Make sure you look particularly at how the data are organised in terms of scale, proportion and time period covered. For example, are they organised in percentages, absolute numbers, in tens, thousands or millions?

- Concepts used in tables etc. need to be operationalised.
- The data have not necessarily been collected by a sociologist, i.e. it is likely that they will have been collected for another purpose.
- The presentation of data can be manipulated in order to demonstrate a particular point.
- It is possible to use data of this nature to identify trends and patterns or to make statements about possible cause and effect.

triangulation; cross-checking; scale; proportion

Qualitative data

- Qualitative data are presented in the form of words and images such as photographs.
- They provide in-depth information on small groups/samples.
- Some sociologists prefer the data to 'speak for itself' — their books contain large amounts of original dialogue/quotations from those who take part in the study.
- Such data are thought to be high in validity because they are presented in the words of those who spoke them. Consequently they are regarded as authentic representations of how those studied see and interpret the social world.
- Some sociologists use open questions and attitudinal scales as part of quantitative data to generate a type of qualitative response. For example, attitude scaling might ask respondents to work out on a scale of 1 to 5 (5 being 'very strongly' etc.) how they feel about a particular issue.
- Other sociologists use conversational analysis alongside observation to elicit qualitative data.

- Qualitative data are generally selected and interpreted by the researcher. This may not be reliable or valid because other researchers may select different types of data or put a different interpretation on the data.
- They may not always be accurate, because they rely on the honesty and objectivity of the researcher, who may consciously or unconsciously select data that support the researcher's hypothesis (bias) and ignore that which does not.
- The data are often recorded after the event, calling into question the accuracy of the recording.
- The researcher may have affected what the respondents have said.
- It is not always clear what percentage of qualitative data collected has been included in the publication of the research.

interpretation; selectivity; bias; objectivity; conversational analysis; attitudinal scale

Questions
&
Answers

This section of the guide provides you with four questions on the topic of **Sociological Research Skills** in the style of the OCR examination. The first three questions are followed by a grade-C and a grade-A candidate response. Once you have thoroughly read and thought about a question, you should spend some time looking at the grade-C response and consider how you could rewrite the answer in order to gain a higher mark (use the examiner comments to help you). Then read the grade-A response. It is important to note that the grade-A responses are not 'model' answers. These responses are not the only possible answers to these questions, nor are they necessarily the best. They represent one particular successful style; one that answers the question set and demonstrates the appropriate skills.

A fourth question is provided which is not accompanied by a student answer. It is followed by a plan of action, and you should use this to write your own response. It is recommended that you spend some time revising the topic before tackling this question. You should answer the question under timed conditions with no notes.

Examiner's comments

The candidate answers are accompanied by examiner's comments. These are preceded by the icon *e* and indicate where credit is due. For the grade-A answers, the examiner shows you what it is that enables the candidate to score so highly. Particular attention is given to the candidate's use of the examinable skills: knowledge and understanding; interpretation and analysis; and evaluation. For the grade-C answers, the examiner points out areas for improvement, specific problems and common errors. You are also invited to rewrite the answer in order to gain higher marks, and some pointers are given to show you how you might do this.

Question 1

Item A

Participation in full-time education, 16–19 year olds

	Percentage			
	White	African-Caribbean	Indian/African Asian	Pakistani/Bangladeshi
Men	43	46	81	71
Women	56	57	66	54

Adapted from Modood, T. et al. (eds)(1997) *Ethnic Minorities in Britain: Diversity and Disadvantage*, PSI, p.76.

Item B

You have been asked to assess a research design. The research is concerned with the reasons why young people choose to participate in full-time education. You should pay particular attention to issues of reliability, validity, representativeness and generalisability. The research design consists of:

- Selecting a school and a college in an ethnically diverse town.
- Informal group discussions with two randomly selected tutor groups — one in the school and the other in the college — to find out what factors influenced their decision to be in full-time education.
- Semi-structured interviews with five volunteers from each of the tutor groups.

(a) Briefly explain the meaning of the term 'representativeness'. (6 marks)

(b) Using Item A, identify two main differences in the pattern of participation in full-time education between different ethnic groups. (8 marks)

(c) Using Item B, identify one strength and one weakness of the research design. (16 marks)

(d) Outline and assess one sociological research method of collecting data about the views of African-Caribbean boys in their GCSE year regarding the employment opportunities available to them. (30 marks)

Total: 60 marks

■ ■ ■

Answer to question 1: grade-C candidate

(a) The concept of representativeness is where people are representative of other people who are being studied. It is important to sociologists because they need to know that their sample is the same as the rest of the population.

question

e Using the word 'representative' in the response to define the concept of representativeness has not enabled the candidate to demonstrate a clear understanding of the concept, but the core meaning is apparent. The candidate has hinted that a sample should reflect the population from which it is drawn, although there is a lack of clarity. An example would have helped the candidate to make clear what he was trying to say. The candidate would gain 3 out of 6 marks.

(b) Item A shows that some people don't participate in full-time education as much as others. The white men and the Caribbean men are lower than the white women. White men are 43% and Caribbean men are 46%, but white women are 56% and Caribbean women are 57%. Also it shows that Indian/African Asian men stay on in full-time education more than any other ethnic group.

e The candidate has identified one difference very clearly in that the data do show that Indian/African Asian men participate in full-time education more than any other ethnic group. A second difference is identified but it is not very clearly expressed, and it over-emphasises gender when the question was asking about differences between ethnic minority groups. It is also descriptive rather than analytical — it is not identifying differences in scale, such as higher or lower percentages. By spending a few minutes looking carefully at the data and then re-reading the question to remind yourself what the question is asking for, simple errors like this can be avoided. The candidate would be awarded 5 out of 8 marks.

(c) One strength of this research design is that by selecting a school and a college in an ethnically diverse town it will be possible to speak to young people of different ethnic groups who have chosen to stay in education after 16 and go to college, as well as to talk to young people who have stayed on at school. This means that the research will include the views of those people who did not want to stay at school but went to college instead. It will get the views of people who wanted to stay on and do a course but did not enjoy being at school. Some of them, especially the Caribbean boys, might have left because they experienced racism from other pupils or from teachers. There is sociological research that says racism does exist in schools, especially towards Caribbean boys. Selecting a college as well as a school will increase the representativeness of the research because some people who leave school at 16 leave because there may be more courses available in a local college than in their school, so doing the research in a college as well as a school means these people will be included, which will make the sample more representative. Talking to people in their tutor groups also means that the research will include people from across the whole range of people in the school and the college.

e The candidate has accurately identified representativeness as a possible strength and has contextualised it in relation to the specific research. The response is accurate, although a little wordy; the candidate displays conceptual confidence and uses a reasonable range of illustrative points.

Speaking to groups of young people is a weakness of the research because if they are with their friends, they may play up to the researcher and tell them lies or not be willing to say what they really think. If they do that, the research would not be valid or reliable. They may lie to the researcher because they are with their friends. This is to do with the Hawthorne effect; they would be changing their behaviour because the researcher was there. Also some people might stay away because they can't be bothered to come to tutor group.

> *e* The candidate has identified a possible weakness but has failed to demonstrate any detailed knowledge or understanding. He has contextualised the response but has left the examiner to do the work. The definition of the Hawthorne effect is accurate but does not apply to interview situations such as this; it is a concept used with reference to observation. Overall, the candidate identifies one 'strength', but the 'weakness' was in need of further sociological development. The candidate would therefore score 5 marks for knowledge and understanding and 5 for interpretation and analysis, gaining 10 out of a possible 16 marks.

(d) The research method that I would use to collect information about Caribbean boys' views regarding the employment opportunities available to them at 16 would be a large-scale questionnaire.

> *e* There is no need to rewrite the whole question; this uses up valuable time. The candidate has immediately identified an appropriate method he would use. That is a sensible thing to do. It is important to spend a minute or two thinking about the method that seems most appropriate to you and which you will be able to write about in relation to the specific area to be investigated.

I would select a number of areas in the country where there are a lot of Caribbean people living and I would then get a list of all the secondary schools in those areas and then select a sample of the schools to use for my survey.

> *e* There is evidence of some understanding here of sampling issues, although the candidate has not explained what particular method of sampling he would use or how a sampling method might actually work in practice.

I would need to gain permission from the headteachers of the schools to send out a questionnaire. They would also need to give me a list of all the Caribbean boys in their school. There might be a confidentiality issue so I would need to talk to the headteachers to explain to them what I wanted to do and to tell them that I would respect everyone's right to privacy and that I would treat everything I found out confidentially.

> *e* There is an awareness of access being problematic. This is a point that could have been developed further. The boys need to consent to do the questionnaire as well as the researcher gaining permission from the headteacher. The candidate seems to have assumed that schools are the best way to gain access to the respondents, although he might have considered other places, e.g. youth clubs and cafés, since this is a group which is the most excluded in many schools. The candidate makes

a brief reference to a sampling frame, i.e. 'a list of all the Caribbean boys', but this needs to be developed more precisely. Does such a list exist? How will boys be selected from the list? Will they be selected randomly or non-randomly? Is there any need to stratify the sample for influences such as social class, type of schools, academic achievement, streaming etc.?

My questionnaire would have open and closed questions in it so that I could collect quantitative and qualitative data. This would make my research valid and reliable. The open questions could be questions such as 'How do you feel about getting a job?' and the closed questions could be about what jobs they are applying for.

It is a good idea to give examples of the types of questions to be used. It is even better to spend a paragraph discussing the concept of 'operationalisation', because the examiner wants to see you discussing how you intend practically to turn your hypothesis or research task into a set of measurable questions. The response above indicates the candidate's knowledge and understanding of open and closed questions. It is a pity that reliability and validity are mentioned together in one sentence, as this demonstrates a possible lack of understanding of these two key issues. It must be made clear how the research is made reliable and valid by the inclusion of closed and open questions.

I would need to think about the best way to give out my questionnaires. I could do it through tutor groups either by asking the tutors to give them out or by going in myself. If I did it through tutor groups, the students might all do it together and influence each other in the answers that they wrote; this would lead to the Hawthorne effect. In addition, there would be people in the room who were not filling in the questionnaire and that might make the ones who were doing the questionnaires feel embarrassed, so they might put down silly answers, and that would mean that the research would be low on reliability. If I did it outside the tutor groups, I might miss some people, and I might have a lot of refusals, and that would also make the research low on reliability. That means it would be difficult to do it again and get the same results.

This paragraph is a little disappointing in its discussion of sampling. It really is not clear whether the sample has been randomly selected or whether this is an opportunity or quota sample. It is important to discuss sampling in a little detail because you are assessed on the basis of your knowledge and understanding of the wider research process, not just on whether you can list the strengths and weaknesses of a particular method. There are some reasonable evaluative points made, but the response needed more sociological substance. For example, the candidate could have thought about how his presence might have affected the outcome of the questionnaires, or made comments about the possibility that questions may have been misinterpreted, or talked about the artificiality of questionnaires etc. The reference to the Hawthorne effect is convincing because this is a concept associated with observation. The candidate has demonstrated some understanding of reliability.

Doing a large-scale questionnaire that includes closed questions would give me some quantitative data, which means I would be able to analyse them and put them into tables and charts. I would then be able to look for any patterns or trends. If I found any patterns or trends, I could then generalise about the views of all Caribbean boys on employment opportunities.

e A useful point is made, although the candidate might have taken the opportunity to be more evaluative with regard to the problem of generalisability.

e This candidate would score 10 out of a possible 18 marks for knowledge and understanding because there is some reasonably sound technical knowledge, but the response needs to be developed further in regard to the specific requirements of the research task, i.e. finding out how African-Caribbean boys feel about the employment opportunities open to them. Conceptual knowledge too is under-developed. The candidate would score 6 out of a possible 12 marks for evaluation because this skill is generally restricted to making some basic points about groups of boys filling in questionnaires. The candidate really needed to focus on the whole research process and use concepts like reliability, validity etc. in a more sustained fashion throughout the response to score higher. This candidate would therefore score 16 out of a possible 30 marks for part (d).

Overall mark: 34/60

■ ■ ■

Answer to question 1: grade-A candidate

(a) Representativeness is when the group that is being researched is typical of the population that is being investigated; when the sample mirrors the survey population. For example, if research is being done on school students who work part-time in the first year of the sixth form, then the sample should have similar characteristics to all school students in the lower sixth — characteristics such as gender and ethnicity and if possible social class, although that might be more difficult.

e This is a well-focused response that covers the issue of a group being typical of and reflecting the social characteristics of the wider population. The example clarifies the candidate's answer. The candidate would score full marks, i.e. 6 out of 6. This question is an opportunity for good candidates, who have done their revision of the key concepts thoroughly, to gain full marks.

(b) One difference is that white men between 16 and 19 years old participate less in full-time education than any other ethnic group, e.g. only 43% compared with 46% of African-Caribbean men, 81% of Indian/African Asian men and 71% of Pakistani/Bangladeshi men.

A second difference is that more men and women of Indian/African Asian backgrounds participate in full-time education between 16 and 19 than white men and women. 81% of men of Indian/African Asian backgrounds participate in full-time education but only 43% of white men and 66% of Indian/African Asian women participate compared to 56% of white women.

e The first difference is very clearly identified, while the second difference is made unnecessarily complicated; nevertheless, the candidate would score full marks, i.e. **8 out of 8.**

(c) A strength of the research is the semi-structured interviews with the five volunteers from the tutor groups. The interviews will provide some rich and qualitative information about how the young people feel about their employment opportunities. In an interview the researcher will have the opportunity to build a rapport with the young people and that will mean that they will feel more relaxed and then will be more truthful in their answers and they might even give the researcher information that he/she had not thought about asking for. Also, as the interviews are semi-structured, there will be an opportunity for the researcher to clarify any question that the interviewees do not understand, which will lead to a much truer picture of how the young people feel. A strength of the research will therefore be that it is high in validity.

e Here is a detailed, well-focused paragraph which makes at least four good socio-logical points about a strength of the research design. The point about the validity of the research is convincingly made.

One weakness of the research design is that it is unlikely that any generalisations could be made based on the findings from either the discussions or the interviews. The research is based on only one school and one college, and in an ethnically diverse town the school may not necessarily reflect the ethnic mix of the town even if the college does. The sample size of the two institutions is too small to be sure that it would be possible to make general statements about the views of all young people of different ethnic backgrounds and the data would not include the views of young people living in rural areas.

e This is a reasonable attempt at discussing generalisability which makes at least three detailed sociological points about a weakness of the research design. The response gets across the issue of sample size as well as the need for a represen-tative sample.

e Overall this is a good response. The candidate has remained focused at all times on the specific research and, although the first paragraph is stronger, this is never-theless a top level response. It would score **8** out of a possible **8** marks for knowledge and understanding, and **8** out of **8** marks for interpretation and analysis, so it would gain the full **16 marks.**

(d) I would use unstructured interviews as my research method since I feel that they are the best way of collecting data on people's views about something. Employment opportunities for Caribbean boys could be a sensitive issue as they would probably know that their opportunities of getting a job are not as good as their white peers. If they do not get a job, they might see it as a failure; it might be seen as not very macho. This means using unstructured interviews would be the best way of researching this group because unstructured interviews are like a focused conversation and that means they are less threatening than other, more formal ways of collecting data.

e This is a clear opening paragraph that immediately contextualises the response and identifies the candidate's awareness of the specific issues that the research group may have to confront and which provides a good rationale for the chosen method. An appropriate method is chosen with a good justification.

I would contact the boys by visiting local schools and youth centres and getting permission from teachers and youth leaders to speak to African-Caribbean boys and ask for volunteers to be interviewed. I would also use the snowball technique which means I would ask those I interviewed at the start to give me the names of others who might be willing to be interviewed. This would be especially useful in contacting boys who are not attending school or college and who do not go to the youth centres, and it would help to make the sample as representative as possible. However, the sample is not likely to be very representative of the wider population and therefore it is unlikely that I would be able to generalise from the data that I obtained. This is more of a case study of African-Caribbean boys in this particular town than a national survey.

e This is a clearly focused paragraph that makes clear how the candidate would obtain access to as wide a range as possible of the respondents. The point about the case study demonstrates an excellent understanding of representativeness and generalisability. It might have benefited from a discussion of why the candidate has decided to use snowball sampling rather than a type of random sampling.

I would need to get permission from the teachers and youth leaders to contact the boys, but I would be honest about what I was wanting to interview them about. I would also tell the boys what I was doing because they would then realise that I was not an authority figure and that would mean they may be more open with me. I would take notes during the interviews because a tape-recorder may be intrusive during what is meant to be an informal interview. I would have to go over the notes as soon as possible after the interview to check that I can under-stand what I have written. I would need to be aware that I may not be able to get everything down and if it did not seem to be working, I might try tape-recording.

e The question of ethics in relation to research needs to be discussed if it is relevant. This paragraph neatly links ethics with access. The issue of the recording of the data also needs to be considered. The candidate seems to be hedging her bets in this paragraph.

I would do the interviews where the boys would feel most comfortable, i.e. in a local café or the social centre at school or college or even a local youth centre.

question

It would be important for me to try to build up a rapport with the boys that would lead to a relationship built on trust. Once I had done that, the boys would feel more relaxed and would be willing to talk more freely and I would then get rich, qualitative and in-depth information. This would enable me to get a true picture of how the boys feel about their opportunities. This would add validity to my study. Since I am close in age to the boys, I should not seem too much of a threat, though I might need to work hard to get them to take me seriously. In order to build up the trust I would have to let the interviews be whatever length seemed appropriate.

🖉 This candidate understands the importance of discussing concepts such as validity in detail. The illustrative material in this section is intelligent and insightful.

I realise that my ethnicity and gender might also have an effect on the interviews; there might be some interviewer bias. I am a white female student and black males may be suspicious of my motives because of my status. Being white may be a disadvantage because my sample may not trust me as they may have experienced racist name-calling or even attacks from white people, which may leave them feeling resentful and non-cooperative. My status as a female might cause problems too because, like males in general, my sample might not want to show any weaknesses as they might think this will affect my view of their masculinity. They might think I would see them as less than real men if they admitted to being upset by racism or the lack of job opportunities. They could put up a macho defence and this might undermine the validity of my findings. However, being as young as them would probably help my case because they could identify with me as a teenager. I would also clearly explain the purpose of my research and assure them of anonymity and confidentiality.

🖉 This is an excellent section that clearly evaluates potential problems with interviewing people who have different social characteristics. There are lots of illustrative examples in this paragraph which are clearly sociological in character. The candidate also offers some reasonably convincing solutions.

During the interview itself I would probe for deeper meanings and explore the boys' view of job opportunities by asking questions that I think would operationalise their concerns. For example, I would ask a series of questions that would explore their views of racism in the job market. This would be difficult to do in an objective fashion so that I avoided leading my sample to give the answers I wanted. However, I would pilot an interview with a black friend in order to see whether I had included all possibilities from an African-Caribbean point of view.

🖉 It is very important to think about operationalisation. You can give examples of the types of questions you might ask as long as you explain how they are operationalising your hypothesis or the research task. This candidate does a reasonable job of explaining why she would ask certain questions, identifying what problems she might face and explaining how she would overcome them.

Because the interviews would be as flexible as possible and questions would vary according to what the interviewee said, it would be impossible for another sociologist to repeat the research again and get the same results. This means that the research would be low on reliability. I would be seeking qualitative data though, and, like other sociologists who seek qualitative data, I would want such data to be as valid as possible even if it meant I had to sacrifice a certain degree of reliability. The objective of the research would be to find out what Caribbean boys' views on employment opportunities are and this seems the best way of gaining a real insight into what they feel. The more scientific and objective method of questionnaires and structured interviews might be more reliable, but it would not be suitable for the type of data I want or for the relationship I would need to build up with the respondents in order to get the data.

e The candidate has concluded with a number of important issues, some of which might have been considered in more detail before the conclusion. One more paragraph that drew the key points together would have been helpful and would have left the examiner with a sense that the candidate had finished.

e However, despite these slight criticisms, this candidate would score 17 out of a possible 18 marks for knowledge and understanding. The research design is well thought through and demonstrates a wide-ranging knowledge of both the research method and the research process. Moreover, this candidate has a very good grasp of the need to apply what she knows to the research task given to her by the question. She also uses technical concepts such as reliability, validity, representativeness, generalisation etc. throughout her response in a confident and convincing way. The one weakness is the lack of explanation for the sampling technique adopted. She would score 12 out of 12 marks for evaluation. This student was aware of the need to be evaluative throughout, to link evaluative points whenever relevant to the technical concepts, and to offer intelligent solutions to the problems she identified. Consequently, this candidate would score 29 out of 30 marks.

Overall mark: 59/60

Question 2

Item A

At Babe, fast-paced music is used to 'create activity' and also to reinforce activity, to 'match fast flow'. There, and in other stores, the staff we spoke with believed that fast music encouraged fast shopping. At sale time, when it is host to greater numbers of customers and more goods are crammed into the shopping space, Mistral uses faster paced, snappier music. When business is slow, shops may attempt to hold customers in the store, to encourage them to look at things slowly, to seduce them into handling the goods, trying them on, and making a purchase. In Babe, young women frequently dance, especially in the changing rooms when they are trying on outfits...A Tom Jones CD sees male customers putting 'a swagger in their walk'; conversely the music of 'a certain country and western artist' empties the store when it is played because it is so depressing.

Adapted from DeNora, T. and Belcher, S. (2000) *Music in the British Clothing Retail Sector/ Sociological Review*.

Item B

You have been asked to assess a research design concerned with the use of muzak in clothing shops in four cities. The research design consists of:
- Selecting a sample of major chain stores and some smaller 'independent' boutiques.
- 50 hours of in-store observation.
- Exit interviews with 150 shoppers.
- Content analysis of in-store music.

(a) Briefly explain the meaning of the term 'validity'. (6 marks)

(b) Using Item A, identify two ways in which in-store music is used to persuade shoppers to purchase clothes and other accessories. (8 marks)

(c) Using Item B, identify one strength and one weakness of the research design. (16 marks)

(d) Outline and assess one sociological research method of collecting data on the shopping habits of young people. (30 marks)

Total: 60 marks

■ ■ ■

Answer to question 2: grade-C candidate

(a) Validity means if the research is accurate or not. It is whether the outcome of the research has been what it was expected to be. For example, it means that if you were looking at whether people were influenced by music in the shops they went to, you find that they did buy more clothes because they liked the music.

e The candidate has some understanding of the term and has given an example which helps to make the definition clear. The candidate would therefore score 4 out of a possible 6 marks. However, to pick up full marks, the responses would need a reference to how the data collected authentically reflect the behaviour and attitudes of those who took part in the research.

(b) One way the music is used is to play it faster and the other way is to slow it down.

e This response is far too brief. There are 8 interpretation and analysis marks available for this part, so it is important to ensure that the two ways are fully interpreted using all the information available in the item. The candidate would score 3 out of a possible 8 marks.

(c) Interviews with 150 people leaving the shops was a strength of the research because those people would just have experienced the music that the shops were playing and would have been able to give the researchers a real insight into what it was like to be a shopper in the shop that they had just left. This would have given the data high validity because it would have given as true a picture as possible of the experience of the shoppers. The interviews were carried out as the shoppers left the shops and so their experience would have been fresh in their minds and, because they would probably have just bought something, they would therefore be in a good mood and willing to answer questions about the type of muzak and whether it made them shop more or not.

e This is a good paragraph detailing a strength of the research design. The candidate refers to the research at all points, although she makes a point in the last sentence which is not based on any information in the item. It does not detract from the understanding the candidate demonstrates with regard to validity.

Analysing the music would be a problem because how would the researchers know what was meant by fast or slow? That would just be their personal opinion, which would be very subjective, so the research would not be very reliable because if someone else analysed it he/she may not agree about what is fast or slow, so it could not be repeated, which would make it low in reliability.

e This paragraph is less well developed than the first, although it is contextualised in relation to the specific research design in Item B. The candidate would score 5 out of a possible 8 marks for knowledge and understanding because the explanations, although reasonably clear and accurate, lack depth and detail, and 5 out of 8 marks for interpretation and analysis. 10 marks would therefore be awarded out of a possible 16 marks in total.

(d) I would suggest that a good way of collecting this sort of information would be by interviews. These would be face-to-face and I would try to make them as structured as possible because the best sort of data would be quantitative. I could put

question

quantitative data into charts and tables and look for patterns and trends on the shopping habits of young people.

e The candidate starts off well by choosing an appropriate method and offering a rationale for this choice.

I would use a combination of closed and open questions and ask them in the same order and in the same way. I would be able to explain what questions meant if some people said they did not understand. Doing that would improve the accuracy of the replies that I got.

e There are a couple of justifications in this paragraph for the use of interviews, but some further explanation is necessary in terms of documenting other strengths of interviews and firmly linking these to the research context.

I think that a good age range would be 16–25 and the best way to find people of this age would be to go to a busy shopping centre at a weekend and use a quota method of sampling. Doing this would mean that I would get a good cross-section of ages within the 16–25 year old range, a balance of males and females and a good ethnic mix. This should make the sample as representative as possible. I would aim to interview 100 young people, which would mean that my sample would be big enough to at least make one or two generalisations. I think that young shoppers who go out shopping at the weekend in one town would be very similar to young shoppers in other towns.

e The candidate has made clear the way in which she would get access to the sample and the sampling technique to be used, although a little bit more detail with regard to how the quota sampling actually works would have improved the marks. Reference has also been made to the concept of typicality in relation to generalisability.

One of the problems of face-to-face interviews is that people may tell you what they think you want to know. Some young people may also lie about their shopping habits; they may want to pretend that they do not go shopping as often as they do since they might think they would be seen as rather 'sad' people. This inter-viewer bias would be affected by my age, gender and ethnicity. It would affect the reliability of the study since if someone with different social characteristics to mine tried to do the research again, people might respond differently. It would also affect the validity of the research because if the respondents had lied, the picture of young people's shopping habits would not be very true.

e This paragraph makes a number of points about reliability, validity and interviewer bias. More marks could have been earned by developing the points in greater detail, particularly validity and to a lesser extent reliability.

e Overall, although the response is brief, it covers quite a lot of key issues and displays conceptual confidence. It would score 11 out of 18 marks for knowledge and understanding because it displays a sound technical knowledge, especially in regard to sampling, although elements of this needed to be developed further to score higher marks, for instance operationalisation. The response is also a little superficial in terms of reviewing the strengths of interviews in the research context. However, it displays a satisfactory grasp of some technical concepts, especially validity and representativeness. It would score 7 out of a possible 12 marks for evaluation because it makes some sociologically relevant points about the problems of interviews. However, the candidate fails to address the research process in an evaluative way — for example, she could have examined the sampling method, the response rate and the interview schedule.

Overall mark: 35/60

■ ■ ■

Answer to question 2: grade-A candidate

(a) The term validity is applied to data that provide a true and accurate picture of the subject being studied. The data are usually qualitative and collected by using unstructured interviews or observations. If a researcher wants to find out about crime in an area, the official crime statistics would not be adequate in providing a complete and truthful picture of the amount of crime that takes place in the area because they would only provide a picture of what crimes had been reported, not all the crimes that had taken place, so the data would not be valid. Another example would be if researchers wanted data on religious beliefs. Data collected on attendance at a church, mosque, synagogue etc. would only tell them who attended the buildings, not who had a belief.

> *e* The candidate has given a clear definition of validity and provided two examples. One example only is necessary as long as it is clear and focused. More than one example takes up time that could be used on other questions. The candidate would score the full 6 marks.

(b) One way that in-store music is used to persuade shoppers to purchase clothes is at sale time when the speed of the music is increased to persuade shoppers to be active and become fast shoppers. The second way is to slow the music down to persuade shoppers to do things more slowly, to get them to handle the goods, and to linger over them, and perhaps try them on and then buy them.

> *e* This is a good response because two ways have been clearly identified based on the data given. The candidate would score the full 8 marks.

(c) One weakness of the research is the 50 hours of in-store observation because observation is very subjective and 50 hours is not very long, especially across four cities. Observation is often done by ethnographers but they usually do it over a long period of time, which gives them time to get into the environment that they are studying. If the observation is done in a covert way, there is a risk that the researcher will become one of the group and 'go native'. On the other hand, if the observation is done overtly, then the 'Hawthorne effect' may occur which means that people may act up for the observer rather than behaving naturally. This will result in low validity.

e This is a clear summary of two to three general issues related to observation, but the candidate needs to link it more closely to the context of the research design in Item B. In order to obtain full marks you should keep focused on the specific research design at all times.

One strength of the research was the selection of major chain stores and some smaller 'independent' boutiques in four different cities. By selecting major chain stores as well as smaller boutiques it would be possible to observe a wide range of shoppers and to record muzak in a lot of different shops. This would mean that the research would be representative of large and small shops and that it would be possible to make generalisations.

e The strength identified is discussed clearly, albeit briefly. Altogether the candidate would score 7 out of 8 marks for knowledge and understanding and 7 out of 8 marks for interpretation and analysis, making 14 marks in total.

(d) In order to collect data on the shopping habits of young people I would conduct a large-scale postal questionnaire in a city that was ethnically mixed. Questionnaires are relatively cheap and easy to administer and would give me an opportunity to identify any patterns or trends in relation to the shopper, which I might want to explore later using another method.

e The opening paragraph immediately identifies the method being selected, which is appropriate, and some justification is given for this choice. There is also an implicit reference to triangulation of data by the suggestion of doing further research using another method later.

I would need to design the questionnaire very carefully to be certain that I was obtaining data on the actual shopping habits of young people. I would need to operationalise what I meant by 'shopping' and by 'habit'. Does shopping necessarily mean that a purchase is made? Does it include window-shopping? Browsing? What is meant by a habit? Is it something that is done every week/fortnight? Does habit mean the same shops? In the same order? I would need to work out the type of information I wanted so that I asked the right questions.

e This paragraph addresses the importance of operationalising some of the areas to be researched, an important skill for a question of this type and one that you will be expected to demonstrate. The candidate recognises the problematic nature of defining key aspects of the research task and would be rewarded for an intelligent list which could become the basis for a questionnaire that produces statistical data.

I would also need to operationalise 'young people'. I would need to know the age group I was interested in because that could make a difference in terms of the sampling frame that I used. If I chose 16–19 year olds, then I could probably use the registers from the schools and colleges in the city. I could then choose a random sample from them and ask the schools and colleges to distribute them for me once I had selected the names. They would not be likely to let me have the addresses for reasons of confidentiality. I would have to pay for the stamps. I would also visit local youth centres and ask the youth workers to distribute some of my questionnaires for me in order to get to young people who had left school.

e Here is another well-focused paragraph which continues to consider the need to operationalise key areas — this time the age group. The questions of sampling, possible sampling frame and the sampling technique are dealt with in a confident but superficial manner. It is not clear how the sample would be selected or how variables such as age, gender and ethnicity would be taken account of.

Mailed questionnaires have a notoriously poor rate of return — only about 30% — so I would offer an incentive to everyone who returned them. I would include a detachable slip with each questionnaire and ask my respondents to send them back with the completed questionnaire. I would then put them all into a hat and send a gift voucher for a local clothes shop to the first name out of it. I hope that one or more local shops could be persuaded to give me the vouchers in return for a summary of my findings, which they might find interesting.

e This is a rather long-winded paragraph but the candidate has engaged in some useful evaluation regarding response rate and the voucher idea indicates that the candidate is thinking through the problem.

The data I obtained from my questionnaire would be quantitative because most of my questions would be standardised, closed questions and pre-coded. That means that I would be able to analyse the data easily using a computer program and look for patterns and trends. Research on shopping habits lends itself to this sort of positivist approach. The information would be as objective and scientific as possible, and the data should be high on reliability. It would be possible to use my question-naire again and repeat the research at a later date, either by myself or someone else, in the same place or in another town or city, and get more or less the same results.

e The question of reliability is dealt with confidently and in the context of the research design proposed. Some excellent knowledge and understanding of the strengths of questionnaires are demonstrated.

If the rate of response was as good as I hoped it would be because of the vouchers I would offer, then my respondents should be reasonably representative of young people, at least in the city where I have done the research, but I think that they would be a fair reflection of young people generally in Britain because magazines and the media have led to common cultures across the country and the shops in big shopping centres tend to be the same. It may not quite reflect young people living in rural areas, but even they read the same magazines. If I got enough back, I could also make some generalisations about young people's shopping habits.

e The candidate has made a number of assertions in this paragraph about the reading habits and subcultures of young people which, without supporting evidence, remain just that: assertions — the candidate's view. However, there are a number of good points with regard to sample size, generalisability and representativeness, and these points would be rewarded.

I would need to be aware that some young people might just throw the question-naire away or lie or it may get filled in by someone else. This lack of response could affect the validity of the research, but if the sample were big enough, then that should compensate for any problems of bias or skewing caused by wrongly completed and lost questionnaires. Interpretivist sociologists would criticise my use of a questionnaire for three reasons. Firstly, I would need to check that the people taking part in my research actually shared my definitions of 'shopping habits' by conducting a mini pre-survey to uncover how young people interpret and define shopping. It would be important that everybody who read my questionnaire shared my interpretation and definition of the terms I used. Secondly, a questionnaire that over-relies on yes and no answers would not uncover the degree or intensity of people's shopping experiences. Even the use of open questions is unlikely to reveal the full details of what shopping means to young people. Unstructured interviews might be better. Finally, the statistics gained from questionnaires tell us little about people's feelings. For example, they might tell us that young people shop a lot, but 'a lot' means different things to different people.

🖉 This is an excellent evaluative paragraph that tells the examiner that this candidate has a very perceptive grasp of the issues involved in researching such a sensitive issue using the questionnaire method.

In conclusion, although mailed questionnaires do have their disadvantages, they would undoubtedly provide me with some insight into the shopping habits of young people. At a later date I could do some semi-structured interviews with a subsample of young people from the same city, which would then give me another source of data, which would be a sort of triangulation. In other words, through interviews I would be able to check that people who filled in my questionnaire shared my definitions and that I had interpreted what they said correctly.

🖉 The candidate provides a well-focused conclusion that draws together the answer and makes suggestions for future work.

🖉 Overall, this is a very good response that deals with key issues of access, sampling, reliability, representativeness and generalisability in a perceptive fashion. In other words, it demonstrates excellent conceptual knowledge and understanding. It is also focused in an explicit way on both an appropriate method and the means of practically applying that method in terms of operationalisation. However, it is in need of further development with regard to sampling. Most of the discussion is constructed around the specific research task, i.e. young people's shopping habits. There is some good evaluation too which goes beyond simply listing the weaknesses of a method. It also makes some perceptive observations about how the method would work in practice. Consequently, part (d) would score 16 out of a possible 18 marks for knowledge and understanding and 11 out of a possible 12 marks for evaluation, making 27 out of 30 marks in total.

Overall mark: 55/60

Question 3

Item A

The changing composition of the poorest 10% between 1979 and 1999/2000 (income after housing costs)

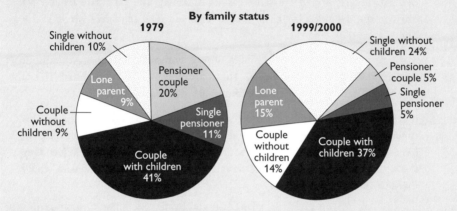

By family status

1979 — Single without children 10%, Lone parent 9%, Couple without children 9%, Couple with children 41%, Single pensioner 11%, Pensioner couple 20%

1999/2000 — Single without children 24%, Pensioner couple 5%, Single pensioner 5%, Couple with children 37%, Couple without children 14%, Lone parent 15%

Adapted from Department of Social Security (1998) *Households below average income 1994/5–1999/2000 and 1979–1996/97*, Corporate Document Services.

Item B

You have been asked to assess a research design concerned with poverty in Britain. The research design consists of:

- Selecting a sample of social security offices in five major cities in England and Wales.
- Distributing a questionnaire to all claimants visiting the social security offices over a 2-week period. The questionnaires are to be handed out as the claimants go into the offices.
- Detailed studies of 30 low-income families, selected by asking for volunteers from the questionnaires.

(a) Briefly explain the meaning of the term 'reliability'. (6 marks)

(b) Using Item A, identify two main changes shown by the pie diagrams between 1979 and 2000. (8 marks)

(c) Using Item B, identify one strength and one weakness of the research design. (16 marks)

(d) Outline and assess one sociological research method of collecting information about the effects of poverty on children in relation to their lifestyles. (30 marks)

Total: 60 marks

Answer to question 3: grade-C candidate

(a) Reliability means that if the research is repeated by someone else, he/she will get the same results. It is also reliable if the researcher can repeat the research.

> Although this is essentially accurate, it is rather too brief. In order to obtain the full marks the candidate should have developed the second point by commenting that the research should also be able to be replicated by the original researcher and the same results obtained. The candidate could have clarified the definition by giving a clear example. The candidate would gain 4 out of a possible 6 marks.

(b) One of the main changes is that single people without children are much poorer in 1999/2000 than they were in 1979. There are now 24% instead of 10%. The other change is that couples with children have gone down to 37%.

> It is important to spend a minute or two looking at the data in Item A. This candidate has thrown marks away by not reading the title of the pie diagrams. He has assumed the diagrams depict whether people are poorer or not. In fact, they show the changing percentage of people in each group. The candidate would therefore fail to score any marks.

(c) One weakness of the research is that all claimants are being asked to fill in a questionnaire. It is good that everyone is being asked to do it but I don't think that it is the best way to find out what someone thinks about poverty. Poverty is a very sensitive issue and can be very personal. The claimants won't know who is going to read the answers that they write so they may not want to put down all the truth. This will mean that the research won't really give the whole truth about the poverty of the claimants.

> This is possibly a weakness, though some candidates could argue that a large-scale questionnaire such as this would be a useful starting-point for a piece of research. Candidates should ensure that they support their point with a good, well-developed explanation. This candidate could have added that the questionnaires might not be completed by the person whom they are intended for, and some claimants may not complete the questionnaire at all. Difficulty with understanding the wording of questions cannot be dealt with by the researcher when using questionnaires.

A strength of this research design is that it uses more than one method. This is known as triangulation and means that the research is likely to give a truer picture overall because there will be quantitative data from the questionnaires and qualitative data from the case studies.

> The candidate makes a brief but sound point. He could have developed the point about qualitative and quantitative data. This response would gain 5 out of 8 marks for knowledge and understanding and 6 out of 8 marks for interpretation and analysis.

(d) It would be quite difficult to do research on the children themselves so I would conduct semi-structured interviews with the parents of children under 16 years old. This would be an appropriate group to talk to since they would know about their children and poverty. This would mean that I would be talking to parents of children who are in compulsory education and are still dependent on their parents. I would use semi-structured interviews because I would want to obtain some quantitative and some qualitative data.

> ℮ This is a clear introduction which sets out an appropriate method to be used and a brief indication of why. The potential sample is well thought through and the candidate is focusing on the research task.

The quantitative data would give me some statistical data which would give me the chance of looking for any lifestyle patterns that might exist in families who are poor. The qualitative data would help me gain some deeper understanding as to what effects being poor might have on children.

> ℮ This would have been a good place at which to elaborate on what type of statistical data might be collected, although the points made about both quantitative and qualitative data are good. The candidate does, however, miss the opportunity to link these points to the concepts of reliability and validity.

I would find it difficult to know who is poor, and who is not, in an area, so I would contact some schools and ask if they would send out letters for me to parents whose child(ren) claimed free school meals.

> ℮ This shows an understanding of the problem of obtaining access to an appropriate sample. The idea is generally good but it needs further development in terms of potential problems such as response and ethics.

I would obtain a list of all schools in the area where I was going to conduct my research and use that as my sampling frame. I would then randomly choose two primary schools and two secondary schools. I would select them by putting all the names in a hat and then picking out four. I would then write to the heads asking for their permission to send out my questionnaire.

> ℮ An understanding of the need for a sampling frame and sampling technique is demonstrated with some reasonable knowledge and understanding of both. There is also an implicit understanding of the need for confidentiality.

Once I had some replies to the letters sent, I would arrange interviews. I would give the parents a choice as to where the interview would take place but would hope that they would agree that I could go to their homes. That way I could see the children's homes and I would be able to put what the parents said in context. It would also help me understand a little more what the effect of poverty might be. If the interviews took place in the parents' homes, they would feel more relaxed and might be willing to be really honest.

question

e The candidate is still focusing on the research task and is thinking through the practical side of the research. He demonstrates an awareness of the importance of location of interviews in order to increase validity.

I would include questions about birthdays and presents, and also family outings and school trips, as well as the kind of diet and the clothes that were bought for the children. If I thought that I had developed a good rapport with the parents, I would ask a very open question at the end about more general comments on lifestyle.

e A good reference, although largely implicit, is made here to operationalisation. The candidate is attempting, albeit superficially, to address the research task and to think about the sorts of questions that might measure children's experience of poverty.

I would have to make sure that my interviews were conducted properly. Some people don't like being interviewed. They might be suspicious of my motives or they might not like my personality. They might therefore not open up to me and tell me about the effects of poverty on their children's lives. This is called interview bias. I could help overcome this by telling people very clearly what my intentions were and trying to make them relaxed. Hopefully this would result in them giving me valid data.

e Some satisfactory evaluative points are made here, although the candidate misses the opportunity to focus on status differences, the social desirability effect etc.

e Overall, this part (d) response shows reasonably good knowledge and understanding of both research method and process. However, more was needed on the strengths of both the interview method and aspects of the research process such as sampling the parents and operationalisation. The candidate also needed to cover technical concepts such as reliability, representativeness and generalisability in a more sustained way to get into the top level of the marking scheme. The response should have been more sociologically focused — it tends towards general commentary rather than focusing on concepts such as reliability. Consequently, this candidate would score 11 out of 18 marks for knowledge and understanding and 7 out of 12 marks for evaluation, making 18 out of 30 marks overall.

Overall mark: 33/60

■ ■ ■

Answer to question 3: grade-A candidate

(a) Reliability is very important to sociologists who want to do research that can be replicated and the same results obtained either by that researcher or by someone else. Questionnaires and structured interviews are the methods that are usually used because they are thought to be high in reliability.

e This is a well-focused response. The candidate would score the full **6 marks**.

(b) The pie diagrams show the changing composition of the poorest 10% between 1979 and 1999/2000. One main change is that single pensioners as a percentage of the poorest 10% have reduced by half, from 11% to 5%. Another main change is that single persons without children now (1999/2000) make up 24% of the poorest 10%, whereas in 1979 they only made up 10% of the poorest 10%. This is a big change and may reflect the number of young people who are unemployed in 1999/2000 compared with 1979.

> *e* The candidate has clearly identified two main changes. She has also attempted in the last sentence to analyse why one of the changes might have occurred. This was not necessary in order to achieve the full marks, i.e. the **8 marks** that this response would achieve.

(c) One strength of the research design is the detailed studies. Such studies enable a sociologist to look at an issue in depth. The researchers would be able to explore the issue of poverty, how the person feels about it and what it means to that person in depth. This would provide rich data that would be high in validity. Detailed studies allow researchers to spend time with the people they are researching and to talk to them on more than one occasion; this means that the researchers would be able to obtain extra information if they forgot to ask about something the first time. Spending time with the claimants means that the researchers would be able to develop a rapport with them, especially as the claimants come to trust the researchers. The researchers would be able to ask the people to clarify anything that did not make sense. It also means that the researchers might find out information that they had not thought of asking about, which would add to the validity and would give the researchers a true picture of what they wanted to find out about.

> *e* This is a detailed answer which demonstrates the candidate's understanding of the strength of detailed studies in the context of this research and shows a confident use of technical concepts such as validity.

A weakness of the research design is that if the research were only done in five cities, it would be unlikely to be representative of claimants in general. First of all, it would not include rural areas, and poverty in rural areas is quite high, so those people would be excluded and it would not then be possible to make any general statements about claimants from the research findings. Second, the claimants in five cities would not be typical of all other claimants. Facilities in cities are different from those in rural areas; for example, the bus services in cities may be cheaper, and there are probably more buses, which means that the poorer people in those cities will be able to shop at big supermarkets where the food is cheaper rather than in more expensive village shops.

> *e* The candidate has a reasonable grasp of the implications of distributing the questionnaires to five major cities in terms of the likelihood of the respondents not

question

being typical of all other respondents. These two weaknesses are dealt with in a fairly accurate and clear way with a confident use of concepts. The second weakness was slightly underdeveloped. The candidate would therefore score 7 out of a possible 8 marks for knowledge and understanding and the full 8 marks for interpretation and analysis, making the overall mark for this response 15 out of 16.

(d) Before deciding how to go about researching the effects of poverty on children I would need to decide on the age range of the children I was researching. I would also need to decide what I mean by poverty and by lifestyle.

e The candidate shows immediate awareness of the need to operationalise concepts.

I have decided that I would look at the effects of poverty on children from 10 to 16 years old because when children are younger the effects might be slightly hidden by the mother making sacrifices in order that the children do not suffer too much, but by the time they get to be about 10, the costs of clothes and other things that they need will mean that it is not so easy for the mother to cover up the effects of poverty.

e This paragraph includes an appropriate justification for the age group to be used and a perceptive awareness of a problem of researching a topic like this.

I would do the study in a town that has a wide range of people from different ethnic backgrounds. I would write to all the headteachers and ask if I could distribute a questionnaire to children in their school. They would probably have to ask permission from their parents because the children are under 16.

e The issues of access and confidentiality are clearly addressed here.

I would take poverty to mean anyone who has free school meals. If the children are on free school meals, it will mean that they are on other benefits too, and that would mean that I was using a government definition of poverty, which might not be the best definition but it is a standard measurement that I could use. Researching lifestyles means that I would need to ask questions about holidays, family outings etc.

e The need to operationalise the terms to be used is identified here. The adoption of 'free school meals' as a means of operationalising poverty is a good idea, although the candidate does acknowledge potential problems.

I would do a questionnaire that would have mostly pre-coded standardised questions so that it would be easy to analyse. I would make sure that the questions were clear and straightforward, that I did not use language that the children might misunderstand and I would also make sure that the questions were not leading questions and that they did not suggest an answer to a child.

e The candidate demonstrates an understanding of some of the problems of designing a questionnaire specifically for children. This part of the question requires you to demonstrate your knowledge and understanding of your chosen research method while at all times putting it into context — in this case, the poverty of young children.

The questions would ask the children to tick their responses to questions such as: did you go on holiday last year? (Yes/No.) If yes, where? Do you have a computer at home? (Yes/No.) Where do you have your main meal of the day? Lunch time at school or evening at home? I would ask them if they get pocket money and, if so, how much? I would also ask them if they work, although I would make sure that this question clearly states that it is only to be answered by those over 12 years old. I would also ask them, if it was their birthday next week, what they might like to be given. I would need to make sure that my questions were very precise and that they were not ambiguous. These questions would enable me to see the lifestyle effects on children.

e The candidate gives some reasonably good examples here, but it would have been useful to have had some justification for their inclusion, i.e. how do they operationalise children's perceptions of poverty?

I would give the questionnaire out to all children in the schools but ask the schools for the list of those on free school meals so that I would be able to compare the responses of those who are on free school meals, which is my measure of poverty, and those who are not. If I compared the two groups, I would be able to begin to know what some of the effects of poverty are on children's lifestyles.

e This is a clever idea. A comparative analysis should provide some very interesting data.

A questionnaire would give me the opportunity of looking for differences between the two groups, but I would need to be aware that the children could lie or, if they did it in a class or tutor group, be influenced by their friends. Also questionnaires, although useful, tend to be a little restrictive when it comes to documenting children's experiences, lifestyles, attitudes etc. for a number of reasons. They don't really encourage the collection of qualitative data in that children may equate writing things down in a questionnaire with schoolwork and fail to express emotional feelings or write down emotional feelings bottled-up inside. Children may link the questionnaire to officialdom and not fully cooperate. Finally, my questions might not fully capture the range and diversity of the experience of poverty for children and I might miss crucial information that would have improved the validity of my study. In other words, I might only get a partial picture of children's experience of poverty.

e Here is an excellent evaluative discussion of the shortcomings of the questionnaire method which is very focused on the research task.

In conclusion, it is not easy to do research on young children, but I think that questionnaires would give me a good basis for looking at the general picture about the effects of poverty on children's lifestyles. I could then repeat the research in other areas since questionnaires are reasonably reliable as a research method. Since I have only suggested doing the research in one town, it would not be safe to generalise from my findings, but if I did more towns and cities and made sure I included rural areas, then it would mean the research was more representative and then I would be able to generalise. If I were able to use more than one method, then I would want to interview some of the children, which would give me a more in-depth picture of their lives and their lifestyles, which would make the research data more valid. Using two methods like this would be a sort of triangulation. The weaknesses of my questionnaires could be compensated for by the validity of the information I acquired from the interviews, which would especially help me check whether everybody who took part shared my view of poverty and its effects.

e This is a good evaluative paragraph that assesses the chosen research method and process in terms of reliability, representativeness and generalisability. It also suggests a practical solution in the form of triangulation for these potential problems.

e The candidate gives a good response which takes account of many of the issues relating to questionnaires and relates them to the topic in the question. The key issues of reliability, validity, representativeness and generalisability are considered, which is necessary for a top level response. The response is a little weak on sampling but reasonably strong on operationalisation of aspects of poverty experience and on problems associated with questionnaires. It would score 16 out of a possible 18 marks for knowledge and understanding and 10 out of 12 marks for evaluation, making 26 out of 30.

Overall mark: 55/60

Question 4

Item A

Activities by gender: how do we use our time?

	Minutes per day					
	Working	Sleeping	Watching TV	Eating	Childcare	Housework
Men	510	510	220	182	88	56
Women	386	450	155	125	175	110

Adapted from UK 2000 Time Use Survey,
www.statistics.gov.uk/thames/social_finances/timeusesurvey

Item B

You have been asked to assess a research design concerned with the time adults spend per week on leisure activities. The research design consists of:
- A pilot study in one town in Britain.
- Using a quota sampling technique to conduct formal interviews with 50 people (25 men and 25 women) at a leisure centre to find out how often they come to the centre.
- Asking 10 people to keep a diary for 1 week recording how they spend their time.

(a) **Briefly explain the meaning of quota sampling.** (6 marks)
(b) **Using Item A, identify two differences between how men and women use their time.** (8 marks)
(c) **Using Item B, identify one strength and one weakness of the research design.** (16 marks)
(d) **Outline and assess one sociological method of collecting data about young people's use of the internet.** (30 marks)

Total: 60 marks

■ ■ ■

Task

This question is for you to try yourself. You should spend some time researching suitable material and making notes, and then try to write the answer in 60 minutes — the time you will be allowed in the examination. Below are a few pointers in order to help you get on the right track.

(a) You need to demonstrate your knowledge and understanding of quota sampling. This means that you will need to explain briefly what is meant by sampling and in particular quota sampling.

question

(b) This is an interpretation and analysis question. Read the table very carefully so that you know exactly what it is showing. You only need to identify two differences, so do not do more than that. Do not try to explain why the data show what they do. There are no marks available for doing that.

(c) Try to write about half a side of A4 each on a strength and a weakness of the research design. Once you have decided what is a strength or a weakness, explain in the context of the research why it might be seen as such.

(d) You should select one method only and focus on it. You must explain why your method is appropriate, i.e. what the advantages are of using the method in the context of the research task given in the question. In particular, you must think about how you would put that method into practice, e.g.:

- How would you gain access to the group you are studying?
- How would you sample them?
- What sampling frame would you use?
- How would you operationalise the research task?
- Would there be any ethical problems?
- How would you present your findings?

You should attempt to discuss these issues using technical concepts such as reliability, validity, representativeness and generalisability throughout.

AS
Coursework Task

In this section of the guide there are two pieces of coursework. First read the grade-C response and the accompanying examiner's comments and then make notes about the weaknesses of that response. Ask your teacher for a copy of the Mark Scheme to help you. For example, has the candidate explained the four key concepts clearly? Does the candidate say how the researcher gained access to the group being studied and so on? Then read the grade-A response. Make notes on what makes this a top level piece of work, using the Mark Scheme to help you. Doing this should give you an insight into what makes a good Research Report and some understanding of how the examiner's mind works.

The Research Report is divided into four sections. Each section has a prompt to guide you in terms of what to include. There is also an indication of the recommended number of words.

Candidate 1: grade C

Section (a)

Please give details of the research on which you are reporting

Title: *Teenage Mothers: Decisions and Outcomes*
Author: Isobel Allen and Shirley Bourke Dowling
Date of publication/completion: 1998
Publisher or source: Policy Studies Institute

e All parts have been completed. In order to reach the top of any level for knowledge and understanding in the Mark Scheme, these details must all be provided.
- If the author is genuinely not known, then you should put 'Anon'.
- The complete title including subtitle should be included.
- The publisher's details can be found on the back of the title page. If you are using an article from *Sociology Review* or another journal, include the title of the journal on this line.
- You must indicate the date of the item you have looked at. Do not claim to have seen Durkheim's *Le Suicide* (1897) if you have been using an extract published in a more recent collection.

Section (b)

Outline of the research design (210–300 words)

You should state the objective of your chosen piece of research, and use this section to outline how the researcher(s) carried out their research. You should describe the aims of the research and the research methods that were used. (You may wish to consider methods, sample size, access to sample, ethics etc.)

The researchers' aims were to find out:
(1) How the women reacted when they found out they were pregnant.
(2) How their families and the fathers reacted and the extent to which they were involved in the pregnancies.
(3) The mother's living arrangements including housing and finances.
(4) The ways in which the relationship of the mother and father was affected by the pregnancy.
(5) The social characteristics of the teenage mothers, including ethnicity, age, religion and whether their own mothers had been pregnant as teenagers.

   e The aims are clearly identified. For this part of the Research Report, bullet points are acceptable. The rest of the report should be written in continuous prose and marks will be awarded accordingly. Some research may have a specific research question and/or hypothesis, in which case it should be included in this section.

The research was based on in-depth interviews with 84 women — 27 in Hackney, 34 in Leeds and 23 in Solihull — who had their first baby when they were aged between 16 and 19. The interviews took place around a year after the birth of the baby. Five female researchers carried out the interviews. Hospital lists from the three areas were used as the sampling frame. For reasons of confidentiality the hospitals approached the potential interviewees by sending letters out informing the mothers of the research and asking them to indicate whether they would be prepared to take part or not. Even if it had been ethically acceptable for the researchers to do this, some teenagers may have been reluctant to respond because the interviewers were strangers. The mothers were asked if the researchers could contact the fathers and the grandparents. Allen and Dowling gained access to 20 fathers and 41 sets of grandparents. The same methodology was used for the fathers and grandparents as was used for the mothers.

e This section does what it is intended to do. The candidate has clearly identified the aims and has briefly described the methodology. Appropriate reference has been made to the sample size, access and ethics.

Section (c)

Reasons for selection of research design (250–300 words)

Use this section to outline the reasons why the researcher(s) chose the methodology outlined above. You should explain why the methodology was thought to be suitable for achieving the kind of data required by the researcher(s).

The feminist researchers chose detailed face-to-face interviews that would give them both qualitative and quantitative data.

e The candidate has made an assumption about the researchers, i.e. that they are feminists, which is not provided in the research itself.

Qualitative data gave more detailed answers, but the quantitative data gave factual information, shown in tables, graphs and charts, which enabled the researchers to highlight any patterns and trends between the mothers and their families.

e The candidate has missed an opportunity to comment on the strengths of qualitative data. A comment on the usefulness of quantitative data has been made.

Although the researchers only used interviews, they asked different kinds of questions, which gave them different kinds of data. Using more than one method of research is called triangulation.

e There is a lack of clarity about the type of data collection and a misinterpretation of what triangulation Is.

The fact that they interviewed fathers and grandparents as well as the mothers meant they could also triangulate the information from the mothers, in relation to ways in which they reacted to the pregnancy and the extent to which they were involved (Aim 2).

e The candidate provides a good link back to one of the aims but is still making inaccurate assumptions about triangulation.

By using a structured interview schedule the interviewers could ensure they asked everything they wanted to, and that each interviewee was asked the same questions. The problem of using this interview schedule is that they may have had questions about other topics that they wanted to find out about and explore with the young women.

e Reasonable points are made here, but the first one needed to be linked to the concept of reliability while the second would have been better suited to section (d).

The fact that they were women researchers would probably have been advantageous as the interviewer and respondent could build up a good rapport and gain trust in each other. The respondent would have also found it easier to talk to women as the researchers would have been able to relate to the issue and empathise with the women they were interviewing and perhaps would have tried not to impose a hierarchical relationship on the respondents.

e The point about female researchers is well made — the candidate is implicitly commenting on the validity of the research. There is some conceptual confidence demonstrated, i.e. 'empathise' and 'hierarchical relationship' are used well.

Questionnaires would not have given the researchers as much detail; no other methodology would have worked well in this research as it was the women's personal experiences the researchers were interested in.

e This is a competent section which misses the opportunity to explain fully why the methodology as a whole was suitable in relation to obtaining the type of data that were being sought. However, some strengths and weaknesses are mentioned.

Section (d)

Evaluation of research findings (350–400 words)

You should use this section to outline briefly the main findings of the study, making reference to a limited sample of the research data to illustrate particular points. (The sample may be attached to the report as an appendix and may take the form of a graph, table, text quotations etc. It will not be included in the word count.) You should also identify the parts of the research that appear to have worked well and those that have not. You will need to show that you are aware of ways in which the methods selected have affected the quality of the data collected and produced, using the concepts of reliability, validity, representativeness and/or generalisability.

The researchers found out that 73% of the women did not plan their pregnancy (Appendix A) but many of the fathers they had interviewed had involvement with the responsibilities and decisions (Appendix B). At the time of the interviews, 43 of the 84 women were still in a relationship with the father. However, many of the relationships did change for the worse or end (Appendix C). The decisions regarding living arrangements were closely linked to the stability of the relationship with the father (Appendix D). Parents and partners often had different ideas of what was best for the teenage mother (Appendix E). 25% of the women were initially afraid of telling their parents (Appendix A).

> The candidate uses appendices to illustrate the findings, but does not always select the most appropriate extract to support the points being made (see Appendices A and B). This series of statements regarding the research findings is a satisfactory summary of the main findings of the study.

The researchers gained a true picture and a deep understanding of what is involved in the stages surrounding and during the pregnancy of a teenage woman and the extent to which her family and her partner are involved. The face-to-face interviews also provided the research with more validity as the women were able to steer the interviews and help the researchers get a better insight into their personal experiences. Female interviewers will have helped to put the mothers at their ease and they will have found it easier to share their deepest thoughts with them. If it were repeated, other researchers might not get the same results. The sample was taken from three major cities some way apart. This could allow the researchers to generalise. The researchers did point out that the girls did not represent a homogeneous group; therefore we could not say the research was representative as their views don't reflect those of other teenage women.

> The candidate identifies successfully why the face-to-face interviews were high in validity and makes an implicit reference to reliability. This section could have been improved by making more explicit references to reliability and generalisability.

What did not work well was the ethical issue of how the girls were deserted after the research was completed. These young, vulnerable women had looked to the researchers for support and advice and suddenly it was no longer there.

■ ■ ■

Appendices

Appendix A

'One woman described her feelings of shock and disbelief: "Really shocked. I couldn't believe it. I didn't think it would happen. I took the morning-after pill and it didn't work"' (pp. 37–38).

Appendix B

'One man described his involvement in the discussion but not the final decision: "I was involved but if she hadn't wanted the baby there would have been nothing I could have done — but she did want it."'

Appendix C

'One woman in Solihull said the father of the baby was a steady boyfriend until their relationship split up after the birth. "I don't want to see him...." "The baby was in hospital, and he [my boyfriend] just slapped me in the face and said, 'I don't want to see him, even if he dies'" (p. 29).

Appendix D

'A woman living at home with her parents recalled her boyfriend's suggestion that they should live together after hearing of the pregnancy. "He said we should try to get a house together. He would get a mortgage'" (p. 88).

Appendix E

'Some parents were quite clear that having a baby was not the right thing for their daughter. "He [her father] said I was too young and had too much of my life ahead of me and it would ruin everything'" (p. 49).

e These are appropriately selected extracts which support the findings summarised in section (d). The candidate has referred to Appendix A twice in the text, although on the second occasion the extract is not particularly relevant. If appendices are to be of value, candidates should ensure they do not just add them on as an afterthought. The candidate has omitted the page reference for Appendix B. Page references should be cited for all the extracts. Using appendices can enable candidates to demonstrate their ability to illustrate the findings in the study further to their summary in section (d). If chosen wisely, the extracts they select can give the candidates added material (not included in the word count) on which to base their analysis of the findings. The appendices should only be used for extracts of the findings of the research.

e **This report demonstrates the candidate's knowledge and understanding of some of the aspects of the methodology used. Two of the key concepts identified in the Mark Scheme, representativeness and validity, have been explicitly addressed in section (d).** (*NB: ask your teacher to give you a copy of the Mark Scheme to help you to know exactly what the examiners are looking for.*) **Validity has also been used in an implicit but sustained way in section (c). Some ethical issues have been considered but they might have been developed further. Reliability has only been mentioned in passing in relation to how it impacts upon the research design and the quality of the data collected. The same is the case for generalisability. Given the nature of the research, the candidate should have considered how reliability and generalisability impacted upon the research design and the quality of the data collected. However, the concepts that have been employed are used with confidence and accuracy. The findings have been clearly summarised and there is some analysis and interpretation of them. The candidate has used the prompts at the top of each section as a guide to writing the report and has been focused throughout on the task. Overall, this report would receive 15/24 marks for knowledge and understanding, 7/12 marks for interpretation and analysis and 5/9 marks for evaluation, making 27 marks in all. Consequently, the report would be awarded 54 out of 90 marks.**

Candidate 2: grade A

Section (a)

Please give details of the research on which you are reporting

Title: *The Lads in Action*
Author: David Moore
Date of publication/completion: 1994
Publisher: Arena

e All details have been completed accurately.

Section (b)

Outline of the research design (210–300 words)

You should state the objective of your chosen piece of research, and use this section to outline how the researcher(s) carried out their research. You should describe the aims of the research and the research methods that were used. (You may wish to consider methods, sample size, access to sample, ethics etc.)

The only aim of this ethnographic study was to provide insight into the activities of the male members of the skinhead subculture in Perth, Western Australia, and to provide a phenomenological analysis of what being a skinhead means to them in terms of their identity. It is based on both participant observation and unstructured interviews. Moore also informs us that he wishes 'to raise an issue germane to a consideration of ethnicity in urban Australia and in other multicultural nations' (p. 2).

e The candidate clearly identifies the aim of this study and demonstrates a confident theoretical awareness of the relationship between phenomenology and ethnography. Two methods used by the researcher are flagged up.

Moore gained access to a 'set' of ten skinheads through Rhygin, a skinhead friend of his. Before starting his research, Moore had lengthy discussions with Rhygin about the skinhead subculture and Rhygin's recent activities. This provided Moore with preliminary knowledge on the subject, which helped him when he began his research, especially with the covert participant observation.

e The issue of access is addressed, which is particularly helpful when participant observation is the method being used.

Moore started his research by accompanying Rhygin when he went out with the skinheads: drinking, talking and playing pool at inner-city pubs and nightclubs, and later writing up notes when he returned home. This was covert research, as none of the skinheads, other than Rhygin, knew that he was a sociologist, thinking him to be just another skinhead like themselves. This enabled Moore to build up a rapport with the set, as they saw him as a member of the group as opposed to an outsider.

e The candidate has developed the point about access, identified the observation as 'covert', and introduced the issue of rapport.

Rhygin would contact Moore whenever he was going out with his set, so the frequency of Moore's involvement therefore matched Rhygin's. We do not know whether or not this is an advantage, depending upon how often Rhygin is involved with the group, which could be more or less often than the average skinhead. After a few weeks of this, Moore revealed that he was a sociologist and asked the skinheads if they would be willing to help him with his research. He then carried out several unstructured interviews with the members of the set regarding what it meant to be a skinhead.

e The second method is referred to and the issue of honesty is noted.

Data were collected over a 9-month period in 1984–85, and comprise information of three types: notes made after participant observation, unstructured interviews and stories collected from the skinheads during the participant observation.

e This is an excellent section (b); it describes the aims and the methods used very distinctly. It details clearly how access was obtained and there is a general sociological confidence in the whole section. This section gives the examiner a good picture of the research, the aims and how it was done.

Section (c)

Reasons for selection of research design (250–300 words)

Use this section to outline the reasons why the researcher(s) chose the methodology outlined above. You should explain why the methodology was thought to be suitable for achieving the kind of data required by the researcher(s).

Covert methods of research were needed for the participant observation as otherwise the skinheads might have acted differently around Moore, if they would let him join the group at all, which is doubtful. This is known as the Hawthorne effect.

e This shows competent consideration of the Hawthorne effect.

Participant observation has always been the central method of ethnographers, as it allows you to observe those you are studying in their 'natural environment' to see how they act. It also stops you from being misled by any false or inaccurate information that the respondents may offer, as you actually witness the things that they say and do. It was also necessary for Moore to establish a rapport with the skinheads before he could interview them openly, as he would need the trust of the skinheads before they would answer his questions truthfully. One important factor in the development of this rapport occurred when they encountered the police while being pursued by a rival skinhead group from the scene of an 'incident'. This shared experience helped to build up this trust, and Moore describes a common experience as 'the most powerful of bonds' (p. 5).

e The candidate very ably describes some positive outcomes of participant observation.

Moore chose a method that would give him qualitative data. As an ethnographer, Moore is interested in feelings and motives, which can only be shown through written data. Qualitative data give you much more detail and insight into a particular subject and a much truer picture of what is going on, therefore making the research more valid, and more appropriate to meet the aim.

e This provides a useful link back to the aim as well as reference to validity in the context of this research.

The use of unstructured interviews as well as participant observation allows the researcher to triangulate data, therefore adding further to the validity of the research. The use of interviews gives the respondent more control over what is talked about, while still allowing the interviewer to direct the discussion and probe for more detail into specific areas, or ask for clarification of certain points. The respondent may also provide information other than that which you have asked for, or perhaps even not thought you might want to know.

e The reference to triangulation is followed up in the discussion of the strengths of the unstructured interviews in relation to this research. The candidate confidently and accurately refers to validity.

By using unstructured interviews Moore is much more likely to meet the aim of his research, as the level of freedom for the respondent to provide information, and for the researcher to enquire further, is crucial to Moore gaining insight into the activities of the skinheads. However, this does raise some ethical issues, as some of their activities, namely fighting and racist behaviour, were illegal.

e The candidate provides a further reference back to the aim. Reflection on the aim or aims of the piece of research is essential for the continuity of the analysis and evaluation. There is a brief reference to ethics, which needs to be developed. The comment on ethics could have been included in section (b) in response to the prompt at the top of that section but would be credited wherever it was located. This candidate refers to it later in section (d). The Mark Scheme is applied across the report, not section by section.

Section (d)

Evaluation of research findings (350–400 words)

You should use this section to outline briefly the main findings of the study, making reference to a limited sample of the research data to illustrate particular points. (The sample may be attached to the report as an appendix and may take the form of a graph, table, text quotations etc. It will not be included in the word count.) You should also identify the parts of the research that appear to have worked well and those that have not. You will need to show that you are aware of ways in which the methods selected have affected the quality of the data collected

and produced, using the concepts of reliability, validity, representativeness and/or generalisability.

Moore found that since most of the skinheads were unemployed or in low-paid temporary semi-skilled or unskilled jobs, they lived at home. Most of their activities took place outside their homes away from any parental control.

Of the ten members of the set, four were English, and their identity as skinheads was often thought to be a 'violent assertion' of their English patriotism. The other members of the set feigned English accents and acted in a very 'British way' (dressing in English clothes, listening to English music etc., as well as distancing themselves from Australian culture). They saw England as the cultural home of skinheads. They also believed that one's identity as a skinhead should come above any other roles that a person may hold. For this reason it was looked down upon to have a long-term relationship, as this is seen as a potential threat to a person's identity as a skinhead. Women were seen as objects to be used only for sexual gratification.

The skinheads placed great emphasis on action rather than expression, visual style (Appendix 1), the importance of being 'hard', fighting (Appendix 2) and loyalty to the set ('Standing with yer mates'). For the skinhead, nights out were categorised as either 'good laughs' or 'good nights', the essential difference being the extent of any fighting that took place (Appendix 3).

🖉 Key findings have been identified and succinctly illustrated in the appendices.

One thing that must be taken into consideration is whether or not the research design determines the findings. Findings may be limited by the aim, with the researcher being 'blinkered' and therefore possibly missing out other important pieces of information.

🖉 This is a quite sophisticated comment on the nature of findings which focuses on how researchers may only find those things that they are looking for, i.e. the candidate is questioning the objectivity of this type of research.

The use of two methods allows the researcher to triangulate the data, thereby making it more valid (giving a truer picture). The use of unstructured interviews also adds to the validity of the research by allowing the researcher to ask for more detail into specific areas or for clarification of certain points, as well as allowing the respondent more freedom in contributing information.

🖉 The candidate demonstrates a good conceptual understanding of validity and triangulation.

Moore admits that he did not use a notebook during the participant observation, 'relying instead on memory for recording events and conversations' (p. 4); this could lead to inaccuracies in the research, although the use of interviews to triangulate data may compensate for this. It is also not reliable, as it could not be carried out again due to Moore's contact within the set. The data collected could be analysed by other sociologists and they would probably get similar findings, although this would depend upon the accuracy of the data collected; however, the use of Moore's memory to record events casts doubt upon this.

e A good evaluative understanding of the concept of reliability is demonstrated here.

Another threat to the reliability of the research is Moore's friendship with Rhygin, which may make his analysis of the data biased, as he is much more likely to be tolerant of the actions of his friend. However, this is a necessary evil, as his relationship with Rhygin is what gained him access to the group in the first place. However, the research is not representative (the information contained in the study does not reflect all skinhead groups), nor is it meant to be. It is an ethnographic study and therefore concerns itself with only one group of people. However, although only carried out on a small group, it may be possible to generalise to other skinhead groups in Australia, if not other areas of the world. To quote Moore: 'Although wary of gross generalisation, the description and analysis of social processes I present is also relevant to the activities of other youth cultures, both in Australia and elsewhere' (p. 2).

e This is an excellent section. Firstly, the candidate weighs up the costs of establishing friendships with members of the group being researched and concludes that the dangers of losing objectivity are outweighed by gaining access to a deviant group. This is perceptive thinking. Secondly, the candidate needs to make reference to representativeness but realises quite rightly that the research was not aiming to be representative of all skinhead groups, although some of it may be relevant.

Finally, there were a number of ethical issues that were raised. Moore engaged in illegal activities. He also observed and condoned, by not reporting, illegal activities of the set. He also deceived the set at the beginning. There are issues about the ethics of research, but Moore would not have been able to do his research had he not been 'unethical', and without his research sociologists would not have benefited from the insights that he gained about this group and their identity.

e This is another excellent section which considers the range of ethical problems that arose from this study and which makes an intelligent and informed conclusion about how ethical concerns impacted on the whole study.

■ ■ ■

Appendices

Appendix 1

'A skinhead cannot claim to be a "skin" if he does not fight. Everything about the skinhead uniform unequivocally signals one's preparedness for violence and one does not don the uniform without accepting the implications' (p. 66).

'Rhygin saw a lad wearing long hair, running shoes, and a T-shirt featuring an Oi! music motif. Rhygin took umbrage at this stylistic combination, claiming that someone with "Hair that long" and wearing running shoes should not wear such a T-shirt. According to Rhygin, Oi! music was skinhead property' (p. 55).

Appendix 2

Skinhead violence — there are three recurring themes in skinhead violence:

(1) The public opportunity to demonstrate loyalty to:

   (i) skinheads as a whole if the threat is from outside the skinhead subculture or

   (ii) to one's closest friends if the threat is from inside the skinhead subculture.

(2) A chance to further one's reputation as a skinhead.

(3) Fighting is an essential part of a 'good night'.

Appendix 3

'The "good night" label is applied to those events which yield social prestige for the skinheads involved in them...who enhance their reputations as "skinheads"... [by]...fighting and being loyal to friends in violent situations' (p. 120).

'Jim...asked me, "Are you in?" I replied, "Only if Rhygin gets into trouble." This satisfied Jim who expressed no surprise at my "only-if-Rhygin-in-trouble" answer' (p. 123).

'The "good laugh" helped to mark the close relationships between friends and amongst members of the action set' (p. 120).

e These are well-selected items of data which support the points made in the findings. The option to use the appendices for data should be taken up, since the data required to demonstrate the candidate's ability to illustrate the findings can occupy too much space in section (d).

e **Overall, the candidate demonstrates a knowledge and understanding of methodological issues at a consistently high level throughout this report. The key concepts have been used confidently, detailing how they impact upon the research design and on the quality of the data collected. There is evidence of the candidate's theoretical awareness in all sections as well as the ability to sustain the analysis and evaluation of the piece of research. The findings have been clearly summarised and the key concepts have been used to analyse them in a sophisticated way. The candidate maintains a focus on the task throughout and has paid careful attention to the prompts as well as to the Mark Scheme. Overall, this is an excellent report that would be well worthy of the full 90 marks available.**

Practice Research Reports

Once you have read the examiner's comments on the grade-C and grade-A Research Reports, have a go at doing a full report. You should be able to get copies of the following three articles which appeared in *Sociology Review* from your school or college library/learning centre.

- Martin, G. (2000) 'New Age Travellers', April.
- Moore, S. (2001) 'Research, reality and hanging about', February.
- Roker, D. (1994) 'Girls in private schools', November.

All three articles are useful for **Individual and Society**. Moore's article is also useful for the Youth and Culture option in **Culture and Socialisation**. Decide which one you will do first. Skim it to give you a rough idea of what the research is all about. Then read it carefully, making notes as you do so. You might want to refer back to the prompts at the beginning of each section (pp. 67–69) to guide you on what to make the notes on. For example, make notes on the aims, the findings, the methods used, the sample size etc. It would probably be advisable to do the Roker article last since you will find that, as with many research articles, the author has provided interesting background material to read first before outlining the research. This makes the article more detailed and a little more challenging than the other two.

Section (a)

Start with this section to help you develop the habit of fully completing section (a).

Section (b)

Ensure that you have clearly:

- identified the aims of the research. This will help you in later sections when you need to refer back to them.
- described the research design including details of the sampling technique used, access, methods, ethics etc. This will help you in sections (c) and (d) when you discuss why the researcher chose the design and how it worked out in practice.

Finally, start to use the key concepts of reliability, validity, representativeness and generalisability if it is appropriate to do so, but remember that there is an opportunity to develop your discussion of these concepts in the later sections.

Section (c)

This section requires you to give reasons for selecting the research design. Avoid simply summarising what the researcher says and consider what you have learnt about sociological research skills. One strategy is to ask yourself questions about the research such as:

- Why did Martin use the methods that he did?
- Why did he decide not to interview travellers on the site where he was living?

- Why did Moore use three young female researchers?
- Why did Roker use a questionnaire?
- Why was Roker so concerned to get a sample of girls from the two schools with similar academic backgrounds?

In this section you should use the key concepts of reliability, validity, representativeness and generalisability to help your analysis.

Section (d)

The prompt at the start of this section instructs you to summarise the findings of the research briefly. In no more than 100 words:
- What conclusions did Martin draw from his research on the life styles of travellers?
- What did Moore find out about the youths who hung around in the village?
- What conclusions did Roker come to about the aims of the girls and their views?

As you summarise the findings, try to identify some appropriate extracts of data to illustrate the findings which you can put in an appendix. The appendices are not included in the word count but do help to show the examiner that you have really understood what the findings are. This section also requires you to demonstrate your ability to discuss the positive aspects of the research as well as the negative ones. You should consider too the research in terms of the key concepts including ethics. Again, ask yourself questions such as:
- What were the positive aspects of Martin's research on the travellers?
- Were there any ethical issues?
- How did the unstructured interviews away from the group he was living with work out in practice?
- Could Moore's research be said to be reliable?
- What sort of insight has the research by Roker given us into the views of the girls?

Use the key concepts to help you to evaluate the research and do not forget to refer back to the aims. Has the researcher achieved his/her aims?

Finally, go through what you have written, referring to the Mark Scheme. Do you think you have reached the top levels for all three Assessment Objectives? Good luck.